R NO MORE ITALIN

TREATING *ADHD* WITHOUT DRUGS

Dr. Mary Ann Block

A Mother's Journey/A Physician's Approach

𝒌

KENSINGTON BOOKS

Ritalin is a registered trademark of Ciba-Geigy Corporation. Ciba-Geigy Corporation has no relationship to the author or publisher of this book and has not authorized or endorsed the contents.

KENSINGTON BOOKS are published by

Kensington Publishing Corp.
850 Third Avenue
New York, NY 10022

Kensington and the K logo Reg. U.S. Pat. & TM Off.

ISBN 1-57566-126-8

First Printing: August, 1996
10 9 8 7 6

Printed in the United States of America

ACKNOWLEDGMENTS

During my journey to good health, I met Dr. Doris Rapp, a well-known pediatric allergist and best-selling author. Her innovative work was a beacon in the darkness. This fine woman and caring physician became a mentor to me in the practice of environmental medicine. I am thankful for her guidance and her leadership.

This book is dedicated to
my parents,
who taught me that you
do whatever is necessary
for your children

CONTENTS

PREFACE

I went to medical school out of self-defense, and in the defense of my daughter, Michelle. She had a chronic, serious illness. Doctor after doctor after doctor prescribed drug therapy for her. Instead of improving, my Michelle grew sicker. I was desperate.

In 1980, by pure chance, I saw a newspaper article about an osteopathic physician who described himself as a "medical detective." While skeptical, I contacted this man saying, "There's no point in us even beginning, if *I* can't help manage this case." He not only agreed, but insisted that he wouldn't have it any other way. I had just taken my first steps toward discovering a program of good health for my child and my whole family—and, eventually, for an even broader audience.

I was a layperson, yet I sought all medical knowledge then available about the illnesses that afflicted my child. Still unsatisfied and wanting to know more, I took an ultimate step: I enrolled in medical school.

This challenge was harder and yet more rewarding than I ever imagined.

As a mother and as a physician, I developed a successful medical approach that enabled my child to grow up to be the healthy, vital adult she is today.

I came to realize that my family was not alone in its situation and its search. That in fact a huge number of families suffer similar heartbreaking illnesses such as those that had robbed my child of good health.

My goal, after graduating from medical school, was to share my medical approach with the people who need it most: parents as desperate as I once was. I opened the Block Center, a medical facility for adults and children with chronic health problems in the midcities area of Dallas/Fort Worth. Before long my phone rang off the hook as calls came from all across the United States. People were searching for an alternative to drug therapy. Soon hundreds of families came to the clinic, and requests for speaking engagements poured in daily.

In 1994 I was approached about using my life story for a "Movie of the Week" project. And I could not have been more honored when my daughter nominated me for the *Ladies' Home Journal* "My Mom Is One Smart Lady" award. We appeared together in the May 1995 issue of that magazine as the grand-prize winners. My greatest success has been the pride that my children, family, and friends have shown in me—what a wonderful validation of my life's work.

Now it is time to extend the fruits of my labor.

This book is one way I can fulfill my goal of reaching out to as many fellow parents as possible. Please know that I've been in your shoes. I know how desperately you want to defend your children against illness and against unhealthy medical practices. It is my hope that this book can help in that endeavor.

Mary Ann Block, DO
January 1996

PREFACE

I went to medical school out of self-defense, and in the defense of my daughter, Michelle. She had a chronic, serious illness. Doctor after doctor after doctor prescribed drug therapy for her. Instead of improving, my Michelle grew sicker. I was desperate.

In 1980, by pure chance, I saw a newspaper article about an osteopathic physician who described himself as a "medical detective." While skeptical, I contacted this man saying, "There's no point in us even beginning, if *I* can't help manage this case." He not only agreed, but insisted that he wouldn't have it any other way. I had just taken my first steps toward discovering a program of good health for my child and my whole family—and, eventually, for an even broader audience.

I was a layperson, yet I sought all medical knowledge then available about the illnesses that afflicted my child. Still unsatisfied and wanting to know more, I took an ultimate step: I enrolled in medical school.

This challenge was harder and yet more rewarding than I ever imagined.

As a mother and as a physician, I developed a successful medical approach that enabled my child to grow up to be the healthy, vital adult she is today.

I came to realize that my family was not alone in its situation and its search. That in fact a huge number of families suffer similar heartbreaking illnesses such as those that had robbed my child of good health.

My goal, after graduating from medical school, was to share my medical approach with the people who need it most: parents as desperate as I once was. I opened the Block Center, a medical facility for adults and children with chronic health problems in the midcities area of Dallas/Fort Worth. Before long my phone rang off the hook as calls came from all across the United States. People were searching for an alternative to drug therapy. Soon hundreds of families came to the clinic, and requests for speaking engagements poured in daily.

In 1994 I was approached about using my life story for a "Movie of the Week" project. And I could not have been more honored when my daughter nominated me for the *Ladies' Home Journal* "My Mom Is One Smart Lady" award. We appeared together in the May 1995 issue of that magazine as the grand-prize winners. My greatest success has been the pride that my children, family, and friends have shown in me—what a wonderful validation of my life's work.

Now it is time to extend the fruits of my labor.

This book is one way I can fulfill my goal of reaching out to as many fellow parents as possible. Please know that I've been in your shoes. I know how desperately you want to defend your children against illness and against unhealthy medical practices. It is my hope that this book can help in that endeavor.

Mary Ann Block, DO
January 1996

SECTION I

WHY I TREAT
ADHD
WITHOUT DRUGS

CHAPTER 1

A MOTHER'S JOURNEY

Michelle's ordeal

My medical approach of treating the underlying cause of the symptom rather than writing a prescription to alleviate the symptom grew out of a personal experience I endured with my own daughter. I learned some hard lessons when Michelle was seriously ill. Drug therapy not only created illness in my daughter, but it also very nearly killed her. The "experts" of traditional medicine had grossly and negligently treated Michelle.

Doctor after doctor lectured me that two-year-old Michelle's bed-wetting episodes were emotional reactions to having a new baby in the house. Even though I felt her health problems were much more, the experts refused to listen. After all, I was only the child's mother, the person who took care of her twenty-four hours a day. What could I possibly know? They were the experts.

The bed-wetting problem persisted, and by the time Michelle was six years old, doctors were performing invasive urological tests on her. The doctors prescribed numerous drugs for Michelle, including Valium to relax the bladder and Tofranil, an antidepressant often prescribed to alleviate bed-wetting.

Our new baby, Michelle's little brother, was six months old when Michelle's problem started. I never really believed that a new baby's presence could actually cause Michelle to have chronic bladder infections (urinary tract infections, or UTIs). Right before the infections began, we had our yard sprayed with pesticides. Michelle developed hives and generalized swelling of her entire body. An antihistamine took care of the symptoms, and the problem was forgotten. But apparently Michelle's body didn't forget, because this appeared to be the beginning of many years of medical problems for my daughter.

Rx for disaster

Doctors treated her with drugs for her UTIs, which nevertheless kept recurring. Our pediatrician referred Michelle to a specialist who began medicating her for her chronic bladder infections. This medicating continued for several months.

At one point in this period, I read an article in a women's magazine about the medication this doctor had prescribed for Michelle. The article said that this drug could cause serious neurological damage. I made a special appointment to see the specialist to discuss my concerns about what I had read. His response to my concerns was to tell me, "Don't read so much."

Shortly thereafter, a new specialist moved to town who had a special interest in this area. Our pediatrician transferred us to him for another opinion since Michelle had not improved. My daughter was seven by this time, and her UTIs had continued to occur despite drug therapy.

This new specialist decided to do more invasive urological testing on my daughter. After he completed the tests, he stated that he could determine that Michelle's bladder was not releasing all of the urine, causing her infections. At this point, he prescribed

long-term therapy with three drugs. He prescribed Valium to relax the bladder, Tofranil, an antidepressant for bed-wetting (also often used for ADHD symptoms), and an antibacterial drug for the infection. Though I explained to him that I did not think she needed the antidepressant for bed-wetting because she did not wet the bed except when she had an infection, he insisted that it was necessary.

Tofranil is often prescribed for bed-wetting because it has a side-effect that causes the retention of urine in the bladder. It did not make sense to me that we would want to give Michelle a drug that would cause her to retain fluid at night. The doctor had earlier explained that Michelle's problem was occurring because of fluid retention. I was just a young mother, and he was the doctor. He explained it away by telling me that this was necessary to help Michelle get well.

Ironically, on this regimen of drugs, my daughter had one of the worst UTIs she had ever experienced. She had hemorrhagic cystitis, which is extremely painful.

This was six months into her drug therapy. When I mentioned her recent horrendous UTI to Michelle's pediatrician, he appeared to become alarmed. He told me that he did not realize she was on all of these drugs for such a long time, and he wanted her off of them. He told me to get back with the specialist to remove her from the drugs.

Michelle goes "cold turkey"

The specialist told me just to stop the drugs. I questioned whether it was appropriate to stop the drugs "cold turkey" because I had observed that when Michelle missed a dose of Valium, she appeared to have withdrawal symptoms. He told me that was purely coincidental: she should have no problems going off the

drugs that way. Once again, I did what the physician said was the appropriate action. I followed the doctor's orders, even though my gut feeling said they were wrong.

Within two days the withdrawal symptoms were obvious. My sweet, even-tempered child was experiencing drastic mood swings between severe hyperactivity and depression. I had never seen her like this, and I was scared. One moment she would be "swinging from the chandeliers," and the next moment she was down on the floor sobbing hysterically.

I called the specialist to report what I was seeing. One of his associates was on call. When I explained the series of events, this doctor patronizingly said, "Oh, just give it a few days." Unable to do much more because it was the weekend, I got the drug inserts from the pharmacist, which detail the drug actions and side-effects. While I did not understand all the terminology, it was obvious from the information printed there that my child was in fact going through drug withdrawal. It was months later that I was to learn that cold turkey withdrawal from Valium can be fatal.

I reported the incident to Michelle's pediatrician. He placed her back on the drugs and began a slow, methodical, safer withdrawal period. But the damage was already done. In addition to mismanaging her withdrawal, the specialist, I discovered by reading the drug insert, should have been monitoring her blood routinely for adverse reactions to the drugs. Alone, any one of these drugs could have caused serious side-effects. All three together compounded that effect. For Michelle, it was a triple assault. Michelle would be sick for the next three years with a low white blood cell count, which could have occurred secondary to any one of the unmonitored drugs. This low white blood cell count caused suppression of her immune system.

The nightmare begins

Before long, Michelle lapsed into a severe form of mononucleosis. With her immune system compromised, my little girl was virtually bedridden. Over the next three years, as I searched for answers to what had happened to my daughter and how it could be resolved, my eyes were opened to the fallibility of medicine.

Looking back on those days, I'm not sure how we managed. I would nurse and comfort Michelle as I took her from doctor to doctor looking for someone to help her. But help was not to be found.

Michelle was frustrated by her limitations. Forced bed rest was extremely hard on my young, active child. She had planned to go to day camp with her friends, but with an extremely suppressed immune system, she could not leave the house. To keep up her spirits and give her some sense of "normalcy," I structured a home day camp for Michelle and her brother. We had daily arts and crafts projects plus several special activities like an indoor miniature golf course that I made with Pringle's potato chip cans for the holes. Our local newspaper ran a story on our "Camp Mono-Nuk-Le-Osis," which definitely earned some smiles and helped ease the pain of isolation.

After three years of taking Michelle from doctor to doctor and finding no help, I was extremely frustrated. Apparently, the doctors were frustrated, too. When they were not able to cure her, they decided Michelle's problem was all in her head.

On our own

I was completely fed up with a medical establishment that seemed to do more harm than good. A friend and I sneaked into the medical library at a local teaching hospital and began to look around. Even with no training in medical research and no assistance from the librarians, we discovered an article in a medical periodical that changed all of our lives.

We learned that mononucleosis could be medically induced through adverse reactions to prescriptions like the ones Michelle had taken. It all made sense. The drug therapy was the reason my daughter was bedridden.

The drugs that she had been prescribed could lower her white blood cell count.[15] With a low white count, the body's immune system would not work properly. This is why Michelle got mononucleosis and other infections and could not get well. The article we found also discussed an association between mononucleosis and leukemia.

My mind reeled at the implications. If I had ruined Michelle's health, it would be called child abuse, and law enforcement authorities would be notified. But for a physician to do this to my child, it's only called "misdiagnosis."

My friend and I flew out of the medical library with a copy of the medical journal article in hand. We drove straight to the pediatrician's office and flagged the man down in his parking lot. The pediatrician continued to be supportive of my efforts. He referred me to a specialist in cancer and blood disorders.

How dare he

The specialist evaluated Michelle for leukemia, a cancer of the blood, and systemic lupus, an autoimmune disease. At this point, I was really scared. Fortunately, Michelle had neither of those diseases. When I asked this specialist if Michelle's problems could be from the drugs she had been on and the way they were managed, he became very defensive. He then quickly decided there was nothing at all wrong with her. He said that Michelle's symptoms were wholly psychological. It appeared to me that this doctor was more interested in protecting the specialist who prescribed the original drugs that started the whole problem than in finding and treating the cause of my child's problem. Later, I was to discover that this doctor sent letters to every doctor Michelle had seen, reporting that there was absolutely nothing wrong with her. But he was very wrong in his opinion, as my daughter continued to suffer.

Michelle had symptoms including low-grade fevers, lymphatic swelling, and infections. She remained on uninterrupted antibiotics for over a year. On the antibiotics she was able to return to school, but if the antibiotics were stopped she was sick again. Even on the medication she could not participate in sports and other outside activities as these things challenged Michelle's immune system even more. All in her head? How dare he!

Medical detective

One Christmas during this period, my husband gave me an unusual Christmas present: a two-volume set of medical textbooks. He had watched me desperately searching for answers to Michelle's medical problems and hoped that I might find something helpful in the medical textbooks.

The next day, during a Christmas celebration at my parents' home, I cleared the dining room table by gathering up the open pages of the local newspaper. By pure happenstance, my eyes landed on an interview with a local osteopathic physician who called himself a "medical detective." The man stated that he liked to find the solutions to medical problems that other doctors had given up on.

I must admit that I was highly skeptical. The doctor I had read about was an osteopathic physician, a DO, and at that time, I had a prejudice against osteopathic medicine, because of stories I heard from others. But then again, I was desperate. I had nowhere else to turn. I often say, "I wouldn't have gone to a DO if my life depended on it, but my child's life depended on it. So I went."

When I took Michelle to see the medical detective, Dr. Gary Campbell, I unloaded all of my frustration about the negligent and insensitive doctors who had treated my child. "And one more thing," I raged. "There's no point in us even beginning, if I can't help manage this case."

"I wouldn't have it any other way," responded Dr. Campbell. And from that moment on, things began to change. I was taking the first steps on the road to good health for Michelle and for a better program of health for our family. Dr. Campbell's medical approach was entirely new and refreshingly different from anything I had heard before. He explained that osteopathic medicine centers around the belief that the body, given the proper tools, can heal itself. (See Chapter 10.)

By the time I found Dr. Campbell, I was ready to give up on medicine altogether. I was incredibly relieved to hear a doctor offer helpful options and support, rather than offer another prescription. He showed me a different perspective. He showed me what medicine could be. Dr. Campbell looked for the underlying cause, he listened to and respected my opinions and input, and educated me by sharing his knowledge. He was a competent and fine physician, with absolutely no arrogance.

In self-defense, mom goes to medical school

But I was still scared about what had been done to my child. I felt that I needed to know what the doctors know to protect my family from anything like this ever happening again. I realized no one was going to care about my family as much as I

would. Though I had been ready to throw out the kind of medicine we had been experiencing for the past ten years, Dr. Campbell was now showing me a different and more responsible way to practice medicine, one in which I could once again have confidence. If this medicine was osteopathy, then I wanted to be an osteopathic physician.

After being a homemaker and mother for fifteen years, I entered medical school at the age of thirty-nine, in self-defense and for the sole purpose of protecting my family.

Though now an insider to medicine, I am still first and foremost the mother who was originally sent on this journey to find a solution for her child. Still, today, the mother that I am guides the pursuit of my knowledge, my medical experience, and my practice of medicine.

While attending medical school, I became very much aware of how Michelle's problems could have occurred. I found out what doctors learn and what they don't learn. Since doctors learn so much about using drugs as treatments, it is no wonder the treatment that made Michelle sick was based solely on the use of medications.

Michelle's outcome

In medical school I also learned how the body works. In courses like physiology, biochemistry, and immunology I learned what I needed to know to help my family get well and hopefully stay well. I also learned about drugs. I knew from my personal experience that I would keep the use of drugs in the proper perspective. I would not forget to always consider how the body works even when drugs were necessary. My medical school actually taught a course in nutrition. What I learned in that nutrition course and also in my biochemistry course was that vitamins and minerals are very necessary for the body to work properly.

Michelle was placed on a protocol of vitamins, minerals, and other nutrients and her health showed signs of improvement very soon after. Several years before, when Michelle first became ill, a friend gave me a book about nutrition and a packet of vitamin C. I remember thinking to myself that this vitamin C wouldn't do anything for my child. I tossed the book and the vitamin C onto a shelf. How ironic! Perhaps if I had listened to this well-meaning friend at that time, Michelle would have gotten well sooner. But she did improve later, thanks to the vitamins and minerals her doctor recommended. Dr. Campbell had a few more helpful treatments. One was osteopathic manipulation. This treatment helped her body's immune system work better and perhaps recover from the insult she had experienced from the drugs. Michelle also had allergies that were suspected to be the original cause of her urinary tract problems. Dr. Campbell treated these as well. It took several months of "detective" work to uncover all of these problems and treat them. With the help of Dr. Campbell and what I learned in medical school, Michelle got well. Today she is a happy, successful adult. Her medical problems are only a bad childhood memory. But the current trend of treating ADHD symptoms with serious drugs is a chilling reminder of the once acceptable treatment used on Michelle. It has helped define my medical approach.

CHAPTER 2

THE ADHD INDUSTRY

JASON'S START

Jason started crying the moment he was born. He didn't stop for two years. The first time he was placed in his mother's arms for feeding, his projectile vomiting reached across the hospital room. When Jason went home from the hospital, he never slept. It was not that he simply had his nights and days mixed up. The child literally never slept! The slightest noise would wake him. And when Jason was awake, he was crying.

Weighing over ten pounds at birth, a fair-skinned, towheaded, blue-eyed child, Jason began his early years with ear infections, asthma, pneumonia, skin rashes, constipation, and severe colic. As Jason grew, the problems grew, too.

In preschool, he spent much of his time in the hallway . . . penance for bad behavior. Jason hit, kicked, and bit the other children and threw things across the room. He picked the worst-behaved kid in the class to be his best friend, and surely that child's mother said the same thing about her son's choice of Jason.

Because Jason could not restrain himself from running out in front of cars, climbing up to high places and jumping off, and other reckless behaviors, Jason's mother greatly feared that he would suffer a tragic, possibly even fatal, accident.

Jason was very, very bright. He taught himself to read at the age of three. There were times when his rages would subside and his parents could see a sweet, lovable child. Yet those times were not often enough. He was shuffled from doctor to doctor, from pediatrician to psychiatrist, from psychologist to counselor. They said that Jason's problems were his mother's fault because she did not discipline him appropriately, or she was spoiling him. Many predicted that Jason would end up in a psychiatric hospital, or worse, in prison.

By age nine, Jason had developed into a hyperactive, aggressive child, seemingly unable to focus on any single activity for more than a few minutes. However, Jason could watch television for hours and seemed hypnotized by the images. He was plagued by violent, abusive outbursts, and spent most of the fourth grade being disciplined in the hall. In addition Jason was uncoordinated and unable to participate successfully in sports.

Doctor after doctor told his parents that Jason suffered from ADHD, Attention Deficit Hyperactivity Disorder, and that the only treatment available was the popular drug, Ritalin (methylphenidate HCl). Even Jason's teacher suggested that his parents do "what all the other parents are doing" and put him on Ritalin.

Although the situation was desperate and miserable and often frightening, Jason's parents refused to accept the dire future predicted for their child: a lifetime of drug treatment and psychiatric care. So they began looking for a physician who would help them find the answers to his problems. Jason's parents brought him to my office.

More ADHD

There certainly seem to be many more children diagnosed with ADHD today than twenty years ago. Today, ADHD has grown into an industry.

Doctors, pharmaceutical companies, psychologists, psychiatrists, neurologists, pediatricians, family practitioners, tutors, and schools all own a piece of this industry. Once a major American industry exists, it just keeps on growing.

With the industry driving the market, the goal is no longer to fix the problem, but to continue to treat the symptoms. This process generates money for those in the industry. If you fix the problems creating the symptoms, all of the revenue-producing drugs and services would go away. There would be no need for them.

Take the tobacco industry as an example. There is such strong marketing promoting smoking, and so much money being made from tobacco use, that it is nearly impossible to make any positive inroads toward improving the health and safety of our population. This is the case even though there is scientific evidence that tobacco is detrimental to the health of our society.

Psychiatric diagnosis

Symptoms now described as ADHD have been around forever. There are many different names that have been used for the same symptoms we now refer to as ADHD. The name of the disorder appears to change about every five years. It seems strange to me that this disorder gets a new name so frequently. Most diseases in medicine retain their names. Cancer has always been called cancer and hypertension has always been hypertension. Why do the symptoms of ADHD get a new name every five or so years?

I have a theory about why this might be occurring. I don't believe the medical community has a complete understanding of this disorder. It is given a name based on the current knowledge. When the medical establishment learns something different about the disorder, they give it another name. These changes occur periodically, so the diagnosis periodically gets a new name.

ADHD is a psychiatric diagnoses, a fact that surprises most concerned parents. According to the basic diagnostic manual used by the psychiatric profession (the *Diagnostic and Statistical Manual of Mental Disorders*, 4th Edition, or DSM-IV), ADHD stands for Attention Deficit Hyperactivity Disorder. The DSM-IV defines ADHD as follows:

A. Either (1) or (2):
  (1) six (or more) of the following symptoms of inattention have persisted for at least 6 months to a degree that is maladaptive and inconsistent with developmental level:
  Inattention
  (a) often fails to give close attention to details or makes careless mistakes in schoolwork, work or other activities
  (b) often has difficulty sustaining attention in tasks or play activities
  (c) often does not seem to listen when spoken to directly
  (d) often does not follow through on instructions and fails to finish schoolwork, chores or duties in the workplace (not due to oppositional behavior or failure to understand instructions)
  (e) often has difficulty organizing tasks and activities
  (f) often avoids, dislikes or is reluctant to engage in tasks that require sustained mental effort (such as schoolwork or homework)
  (g) often loses things necessary for tasks or activities (e.g., toys, school assignments, pencils, books or tools)
  (h) is often easily distracted by extraneous stimuli
  (i) is often forgetful in daily activities

  (2) six (or more) of the following symptoms of hyperactivity-impulsivity have persisted for at least 6 months to a degree that is maladaptive and inconsistent with developmental level:

Hyperactivity

(a) often fidgets with hands or feet or squirms in seat

(b) often leaves seat in classroom or in other situations in which remaining in seat is expected

(c) often runs about or climbs excessively in situations in which it is inappropriate (in adolescents or adults, may be limited to subjective feelings of restlessness)

(d) often has difficulty playing or engaging in leisure activities quietly

(e) is often "on the go" or often acts as if "driven by a motor"

(f) often talks excessively

Impulsivity

(g) often blurts out answers before questions have been completed

(h) often has difficulty awaiting turn

(i) often interrupts or intrudes on others (e.g., butts into conversations or games)

B. Some hyperactive-impulsive or inattentive symptoms that caused impairment were present before age 7 years.

C. Some impairment from the symptoms is present in two or more settings (e.g., at school [or work] and at home)

D. There must be clear evidence of clinically significant impairment in social, academic or occupational functioning.

E. The symptoms do not occur exclusively during the course of a Pervasive Developmental Disorder, Schizophrenia or other Psychotic Disorder and are not better accounted for by another mental disorder (e.g., Mood Disorder, Anxiety Disorder, Dissociative Disorder or a Personality Disorder).[1]

Subjective symptoms

Look closely at the actual wording of the DSM-IV diagnosis. The symptoms of ADHD are highly subjective. The chance that your child will or will not receive a diagnosis of ADHD depends upon the point of view of the individual making the evaluation.

If the evaluator believes that a child should be seen and not heard and should be able to remain seated for long periods of time, then the child is more likely to receive an ADHD diagnosis.

However, if the evaluator thinks that children should be allowed to act like children, speaking out and moving about, then the child is less likely to receive such a diagnosis. The child must have at least six of the symptoms to receive the diagnosis. However it shouldn't matter if a child has one symptom or twelve symptoms. If her or his behavior interferes with life at home or in school, the child needs help. Giving the child a label and a drug is not what I think that help should be.

ADHD is not a new disorder

The symptoms of ADHD have always been present in children. It does appear that this label is now being applied to more children than ever before. While it has been stated that about three percent of children manifest the ADHD symptoms, six percent are actually on medications for ADHD.[6]

ADHD is the latest in a long line of names given to the diagnosis for this group of symptoms. Others include:

- Minimal Brain Dysfunction
- Hyperkinetic Child Syndrome
- Hyperactivity
- Minor Cerebral Dysfunction
- Attention Deficit Disorder (with and without Hyperactivity)
- Attention Deficit Hyperactivity Disorder
- Attention Deficit/Hyperactivity Disorder, Combined, Predominately Inattentive Type or Predominately Hyperactive-Impulsive Type

JASON'S OUTCOME

Many children who have been diagnosed with ADHD have a similar infant history as Jason: colic, crying, insomnia, ear infections, and temper tantrums. Some of these symptoms relate to low blood sugar and some to allergies or hypersensitivities.

The underlying cause of Jason's symptoms, which had been diagnosed as ADHD, was actually food sensitivities and hypoglycemia, also known as low blood sugar. Modifying his diet corrected the behavior problem. The effects of low blood sugar on behavior will be discussed more thoroughly in Chapter 6. With Jason's behavior problems resolved, his personality changed dramatically. He is now a sweet, thoughtful, considerate young man. The teenage years, which his parents had anticipated with fear prior to his treatment for hypoglycemia, were delightful. Jason's learning problems were treated with the Learn-How-To-Learn™ program, which is available through the Block Center (see Chapter 8). He eventually obtained exceptional grades and excelled in sports. Jason didn't have ADHD. He had hypoglycemia, food sensitivities, and learning disabilities.

Attention deficit disorder and hyperactivity are different

I definitely prefer not to label anyone, but if I had to choose from all of the names used thus far, I would prefer "Attention Deficit Disorder with or without Hyperactivity." I believe that throwing the two diagnoses together as ADHD tends to confuse things. If the two disorders are classified as one, it will be much more difficult to find the underlying causes.

From a physiological perspective, I believe the two disorders stem from two very different underlying problems. The two disorders certainly manifest themselves differently, meaning that the afflicted children present very different symptoms.

"Attention deficit predominately inattentive"

Attention Deficit Predominately Inattentive is the term used in the DSM-IV to describe the child who is not hyperactive. I think the child who has Attention Deficit Disorder without hyperactivity or behavior problems usually has a "processing" problem. This child's problems usually show up in about the fourth or fifth grade, but can show up earlier. Because they do not misbehave, their problems often go unnoticed for years. They are often quiet, and though intelligent, just do not do well in school. These children cannot seem to take in the information that is presented to them even though they are quite bright. Processing, or how the brain takes in information and interprets it, may be the only problem. (Chapter 8, Learn-How-To-Learn, will explain how to deal with this problem.)

"Attention deficit predominately hyperactive-impulsive"

This diagnosis from the DSM-IV is often applied to the child who can't sit still, can't pay attention, and is often a behavioral problem according to the teacher and often the parents. Teachers, therapists, and medical professionals who believe ADHD exists will make a diagnosis in a variety of ways. Using the subjective symptoms listed in the DSM-IV, anyone can easily determine if a child meets the criteria. What is even more puzzling, however, is that in spite of the fact that there are these simple subjective diagnostic criteria, many therapists have begun to use some psychological tests for their evaluation. Testing for ADHD, in my opinion, has developed in recent years in a weak attempt to objectify an entirely subjective diagnosis. ADHD cannot be diagnosed objectively. At present, there is no biochemical marker established that is specific to the ADHD child. We can't draw blood, run a test, and say, "Your child has ADHD."

Instead, the testing that has been developed is supposed to determine if a child can concentrate and hold attention throughout certain activities. Once again, this conveys little, if any, objective information. Parents can spend thousands of dollars for one of these evaluations to get the same diagnosis or label that they could get for much less. After spending all that money for the label of ADHD, parents must then see a physician for medication. I prefer to look into the types of problems the child is having and then ask some meaningful questions. What is the underlying cause of the problem? Can it be determined? If so, can it be fixed?

Because there may be other psychological and learning problems to rule out, having an evaluation administered by a psychologist may be important. But when doctors hear that the child is having behavioral problems or attention problems, they

will often just reach for the prescription pad. Other [problems] may be overlooked. A thorough medical exam[ination] and evaluation is very important. Too many children I ha[ve] have not had such a medical evaluation. Today, with [us] using the HMO model of medicine, I know that even le[ss thor]ough evaluations are being done. Too often, when a chil[d has]ing ADHD-type problems, it is just assumed that it is [ADHD] and medication is prescribed.

I personally do not know why it is important to d[iagnose] ADHD, but it appears that the diagnosis allows doctors [to write] a prescription of methylphenidate HCl (Ritalin) or som[e other] medication to treat the symptom.

Parents frequently tell me that their child has been tes[ted and] determined to be "borderline" ADHD because their ch[ild has] only one or two of the eighteen ADHD symptoms. This d[iagnosis] of borderline ADHD conveys little, if any, meaningful i[nforma]tion.

To me it does not matter if the child has all eightee[n symp]toms or only one of them. If the child is having problem[s in any] area of her or his life—school, home, sports, or other acti[vity—] the problem should be addressed.

This is one of the many reasons that I do not use the [ADHD] diagnosis in my practice at the Block Center. All it doe[s is label] the child with a psychiatric diagnosis and give permiss[ion to a] physician to write a prescription for drugs. It can also [give] parents and the child a reason or excuse for why the chi[ld isn't] successful.

So now we have an ADHD industry. The people runn[ing the] industry are making a great deal of money from it. I woul[d not ob]ject to money being made if the problem were actually be[ing helped] or cured. Unfortunately that's not the case. Since the [primary] treatment of ADHD is drugs, let's take a hard look at dr[ugs.]

CHAPTER 3

IT'S ALL ABOUT DRUGS

Current treatment for ADHD

The most common treatment for ADHD in America today is drug therapy. Even the historical treatment is supposed to combine drugs, behavioral modification, and educational services. However, studies indicate that pediatricians are more likely to prescribe mainly drugs, without the other two treatments. About 80 to 85 percent of ADHD children receive drugs, while only about half of that number receive behavioral and educational modifications.[2] Interestingly, medical literature reveals that family practitioners do a better job of prescribing some behavioral and educational modifications for ADHD children than do pediatricians.[3]

Ritalin, the most commonly prescribed drug for ADHD symptoms, is one of many other drugs currently used to treat ADHD. The list includes dextroamphetamine (Dexedrine), pemoline (Cylert), imipramine hydrochloride (Tofranil), desipramine (Norpramin), various antiseizure medications, and clonidine (Catapres), Prozac, and Paxil.

Ritalin is being prescribed in such vast amounts, that in December 1993, Ciba-Geigy, the company that manufactures the drug, ran out of pills. Ritalin is a controlled substance, like morphine. The controlled substance designation means that there is concern by the Drug Enforcement Agency (DEA) that the drug has potential for abuse and/or addiction. Because it is a controlled substance, doctors must keep very careful records when they prescribe it. Doctors must use a standard triplicate prescription form, with an original and two copies. One copy is retained by the doctor, another goes to the pharmacist, and another to the DEA. The DEA tracks where and when the drug has been prescribed and dispensed. If it is being prescribed or dispensed too often, abuse may be occurring.

The DEA puts manufacturing limits on controlled substances. A pharmaceutical company is allowed to make only a certain amount of the drug each year. And all of the drug must be accounted for. In 1993 the allotment for Ritalin ran out before the year was over. Ciba-Geigy could not begin to manufacture more until 1994 unless granted special permission by the DEA. The 1993 Ritalin shortfall caused a virtual panic among many parents of children who are dependent on Ritalin as their only treatment. The situation received intense media attention.

In my opinion, however, the popularity of a treatment is no indication of its merit. In fact, popularity may even prevent us from focusing beyond the quick fix to seek the underlying cause of the problem.

I am concerned that we will never really understand a child's underlying health problems if we look at the child's illness from the perspective of how best to treat the symptoms with drugs. Instead, my philosophy and approach is that we must identify and treat the underlying cause of the problem, not symptoms such as hyperactivity, aggressive behavior, and poor attention.

It is ironic to me that doctors today do not like the power and control insurance companies are exerting over them, while doctors have been controlled for over fifty years by the drug companies.

Yes, the drug companies control medicine and the way doctors practice. They control medical schools, continuing medical education, medical journals, and medical research.

Doctors didn't mind when it was just drug companies controlling medicine. It was a symbiotic relationship. The drug companies made money by helping the doctors make money. Now insurance companies are making money by decreasing the doctors' income, so the doctors object. It is the same with ADHD. The drug companies are making so much money from the diagnosis and treatment of ADHD that even if the drugs are shown not to be the best treatment, drug treatment will not go away.

Todd Forte, a spokesperson for Ciba-Geigy, the company that makes Ritalin, has said that over three million people are currently taking Ritalin. Most are children. CHADD (Children and Adults with ADD), a national support group for ADHD that has been a very vocal advocate for the use of Ritalin and other drugs for the treatment of ADHD, was exposed recently for its close relationship with the drug companies. ABC television revealed on *20/20* (October 27, 1995) that CHADD has received over $800,000 from Ciba-Geigy, the company that makes Ritalin. CHADD has even petitioned the Drug Enforcement Agency (DEA) to remove Ritalin from its controlled substance status. Such removal would make it easier for doctors to write prescriptions for Ritalin, expanding the use of the drug.

If three million people are on Ritalin, imagine the profit for that drug company. A conservative estimate would put the cost per month of Ritalin, methylphenidate HCl, at $30. It is an immense revenue stream: $30 per month for three million people would create revenues of over $1 billion for one drug company in one year alone. Add in the cost of the other drugs that are used plus educational, psychological, medical, and other professional fees. The total will easily exceed $2 billion per year.

That's how the ADHD industry has grown. The more ADHD diagnoses, the more drugs are prescribed, the more services are provided, the more jobs people have, and the more money everyone in the ADHD industry makes. Where is the motivation for those making the money in the industry to come up with a better solution to the problem unless the solution enhances their financial position? What a comfortable situation for everyone in the ADHD industry. They all make a lot of money while appearing to be helpful. No one is actually getting well, so the money never stops. While all those working successfully in the ADHD industry are making money, your child could be losing out on good health, missing a drug-free childhood, and losing an opportunity to reach her or his full potential.

Why is ADHD treated so frequently with drugs?

The drug Ritalin has been used for many years for the treatment of behavior problems in children. At first the drug was thought to have a paradoxical effect on children with ADHD. It was thought that children with ADHD had "some of their wires crossed." Even though Ritalin and other amphetamine-like drugs were "uppers" for most people, in these children, the drug was thought to have an opposite effect and actually calm them down. Then about ten to fifteen years ago, the research in the area led to a more comprehensive understanding of the mechanism of amphetamine action. Experts determined that the drug actually was not paradoxical, but in fact did the same thing to these children as it did to normal children and adults. The drug, in essence, helped them "focus."

Attention deficit disorder and hyperactivity are different

I definitely prefer not to label anyone, but if I had to choose from all of the names used thus far, I would prefer "Attention Deficit Disorder with or without Hyperactivity." I believe that throwing the two diagnoses together as ADHD tends to confuse things. If the two disorders are classified as one, it will be much more difficult to find the underlying causes.

From a physiological perspective, I believe the two disorders stem from two very different underlying problems. The two disorders certainly manifest themselves differently, meaning that the afflicted children present very different symptoms.

"Attention deficit predominately inattentive"

Attention Deficit Predominately Inattentive is the term used in the DSM-IV to describe the child who is not hyperactive. I think the child who has Attention Deficit Disorder without hyperactivity or behavior problems usually has a "processing" problem. This child's problems usually show up in about the fourth or fifth grade, but can show up earlier. Because they do not misbehave, their problems often go unnoticed for years. They are often quiet, and though intelligent, just do not do well in school. These children cannot seem to take in the information that is presented to them even though they are quite bright. Processing, or how the brain takes in information and interprets it, may be the only problem. (Chapter 8, Learn-How-To-Learn, will explain how to deal with this problem.)

"Attention deficit predominately hyperactive-impulsive"

This diagnosis from the DSM-IV is often applied to the child who can't sit still, can't pay attention, and is often a behavioral problem according to the teacher and often the parents. Teachers, therapists, and medical professionals who believe ADHD exists will make a diagnosis in a variety of ways. Using the subjective symptoms listed in the DSM-IV, anyone can easily determine if a child meets the criteria. What is even more puzzling, however, is that in spite of the fact that there are these simple subjective diagnostic criteria, many therapists have begun to use some psychological tests for their evaluation. Testing for ADHD, in my opinion, has developed in recent years in a weak attempt to objectify an entirely subjective diagnosis. ADHD cannot be diagnosed objectively. At present, there is no biochemical marker established that is specific to the ADHD child. We can't draw blood, run a test, and say, "Your child has ADHD."

Instead, the testing that has been developed is supposed to determine if a child can concentrate and hold attention throughout certain activities. Once again, this conveys little, if any, objective information. Parents can spend thousands of dollars for one of these evaluations to get the same diagnosis or label that they could get for much less. After spending all that money for the label of ADHD, parents must then see a physician for medication. I prefer to look into the types of problems the child is having and then ask some meaningful questions. What is the underlying cause of the problem? Can it be determined? If so, can it be fixed?

Because there may be other psychological and learning problems to rule out, having an evaluation administered by a psychologist may be important. But when doctors hear that the child is having behavioral problems or attention problems, they will often just reach for the prescription pad. Other medical problems may be overlooked. A thorough medical examination and evaluation is very important. Too many children I have seen have not had such a medical evaluation. Today, with people using the HMO model of medicine, I know that even less thorough evaluations are being done. Too often, when a child is having ADHD-type problems, it is just assumed that it is ADHD, and medication is prescribed.

I personally do not know why it is important to diagnose ADHD, but it appears that the diagnosis allows doctors to give a prescription of methylphenidate HCl (Ritalin) or some other medication to treat the symptom.

Parents frequently tell me that their child has been tested and determined to be "borderline" ADHD because their child had only one or two of the eighteen ADHD symptoms. This diagnosis of borderline ADHD conveys little, if any, meaningful information.

To me it does not matter if the child has all eighteen symptoms or only one of them. If the child is having problems in any area of her or his life—school, home, sports, or other activities— the problem should be addressed.

This is one of the many reasons that I do not use the ADHD diagnosis in my practice at the Block Center. All it does is label the child with a psychiatric diagnosis and give permission to a physician to write a prescription for drugs. It can also give the parents and the child a reason or excuse for why the child is not successful.

So now we have an ADHD industry. The people running this industry are making a great deal of money from it. I would not object to money being made if the problem were actually being fixed or cured. Unfortunately that's not the case. Since the primary treatment of ADHD is drugs, let's take a hard look at drugs next.

JASON'S OUTCOME

Many children who have been diagnosed with ADHD have a similar infant history as Jason: colic, crying, insomnia, ear infections, and temper tantrums. Some of these symptoms relate to low blood sugar and some to allergies or hypersensitivities.

The underlying cause of Jason's symptoms, which had been diagnosed as ADHD, was actually food sensitivities and hypoglycemia, also known as low blood sugar. Modifying his diet corrected the behavior problem. The effects of low blood sugar on behavior will be discussed more thoroughly in Chapter 6. With Jason's behavior problems resolved, his personality changed dramatically. He is now a sweet, thoughtful, considerate young man. The teenage years, which his parents had anticipated with fear prior to his treatment for hypoglycemia, were delightful. Jason's learning problems were treated with the Learn-How-To-Learn™ program, which is available through the Block Center (see Chapter 8). He eventually obtained exceptional grades and excelled in sports. Jason didn't have ADHD. He had hypoglycemia, food sensitivities, and learning disabilities.

CHAPTER 3

IT'S ALL ABOUT DRUGS

Current treatment for ADHD

The most common treatment for ADHD in America today is drug therapy. Even the historical treatment is supposed to combine drugs, behavioral modification, and educational services. However, studies indicate that pediatricians are more likely to prescribe mainly drugs, without the other two treatments. About 80 to 85 percent of ADHD children receive drugs, while only about half of that number receive behavioral and educational modifications.[2] Interestingly, medical literature reveals that family practitioners do a better job of prescribing some behavioral and educational modifications for ADHD children than do pediatricians.[3]

Ritalin, the most commonly prescribed drug for ADHD symptoms, is one of many other drugs currently used to treat ADHD. The list includes dextroamphetamine (Dexedrine), pemoline (Cylert), imipramine hydrochloride (Tofranil), desipramine (Norpramin), various antiseizure medications, and clonidine (Catapres), Prozac, and Paxil.

Ritalin is being prescribed in such vast amounts, that in December 1993, Ciba-Geigy, the company that manufactures the drug, ran out of pills. Ritalin is a controlled substance, like morphine. The controlled substance designation means that there is concern by the Drug Enforcement Agency (DEA) that the drug has potential for abuse and/or addiction. Because it is a controlled substance, doctors must keep very careful records when they prescribe it. Doctors must use a standard triplicate prescription form, with an original and two copies. One copy is retained by the doctor, another goes to the pharmacist, and another to the DEA. The DEA tracks where and when the drug has been prescribed and dispensed. If it is being prescribed or dispensed too often, abuse may be occurring.

The DEA puts manufacturing limits on controlled substances. A pharmaceutical company is allowed to make only a certain amount of the drug each year. And all of the drug must be accounted for. In 1993 the allotment for Ritalin ran out before the year was over. Ciba-Geigy could not begin to manufacture more until 1994 unless granted special permission by the DEA. The 1993 Ritalin shortfall caused a virtual panic among many parents of children who are dependent on Ritalin as their only treatment. The situation received intense media attention.

In my opinion, however, the popularity of a treatment is no indication of its merit. In fact, popularity may even prevent us from focusing beyond the quick fix to seek the underlying cause of the problem.

I am concerned that we will never really understand a child's underlying health problems if we look at the child's illness from the perspective of how best to treat the symptoms with drugs. Instead, my philosophy and approach is that we must identify and treat the underlying cause of the problem, not symptoms such as hyperactivity, aggressive behavior, and poor attention.

It is ironic to me that doctors today do not like the power and control insurance companies are exerting over them, while doctors have been controlled for over fifty years by the drug companies.

Yes, the drug companies control medicine and the way doctors practice. They control medical schools, continuing medical education, medical journals, and medical research.

Doctors didn't mind when it was just drug companies controlling medicine. It was a symbiotic relationship. The drug companies made money by helping the doctors make money. Now insurance companies are making money by decreasing the doctors' income, so the doctors object. It is the same with ADHD. The drug companies are making so much money from the diagnosis and treatment of ADHD that even if the drugs are shown not to be the best treatment, drug treatment will not go away.

Todd Forte, a spokesperson for Ciba-Geigy, the company that makes Ritalin, has said that over three million people are currently taking Ritalin. Most are children. CHADD (Children and Adults with ADD), a national support group for ADHD that has been a very vocal advocate for the use of Ritalin and other drugs for the treatment of ADHD, was exposed recently for its close relationship with the drug companies. ABC television revealed on 20/20 (October 27, 1995) that CHADD has received over $800,000 from Ciba-Geigy, the company that makes Ritalin. CHADD has even petitioned the Drug Enforcement Agency (DEA) to remove Ritalin from its controlled substance status. Such removal would make it easier for doctors to write prescriptions for Ritalin, expanding the use of the drug.

If three million people are on Ritalin, imagine the profit for that drug company. A conservative estimate would put the cost per month of Ritalin, methylphenidate HCl, at $30. It is an immense revenue stream: $30 per month for three million people would create revenues of over $1 billion for one drug company in one year alone. Add in the cost of the other drugs that are used plus educational, psychological, medical, and other professional fees. The total will easily exceed $2 billion per year.

That's how the ADHD industry has grown. The more ADHD diagnoses, the more drugs are prescribed, the more services are provided, the more jobs people have, and the more money everyone in the ADHD industry makes. Where is the motivation for those making the money in the industry to come up with a better solution to the problem unless the solution enhances their financial position? What a comfortable situation for everyone in the ADHD industry. They all make a lot of money while appearing to be helpful. No one is actually getting well, so the money never stops. While all those working successfully in the ADHD industry are making money, your child could be losing out on good health, missing a drug-free childhood, and losing an opportunity to reach her or his full potential.

Why is ADHD treated so frequently with drugs?

The drug Ritalin has been used for many years for the treatment of behavior problems in children. At first the drug was thought to have a paradoxical effect on children with ADHD. It was thought that children with ADHD had "some of their wires crossed." Even though Ritalin and other amphetamine-like drugs were "uppers" for most people, in these children, the drug was thought to have an opposite effect and actually calm them down. Then about ten to fifteen years ago, the research in the area led to a more comprehensive understanding of the mechanism of amphetamine action. Experts determined that the drug actually was not paradoxical, but in fact did the same thing to these children as it did to normal children and adults. The drug, in essence, helped them "focus."

market actually cure anything. Drugs simply cover up symptoms; they do not cure.

Can't you stay on medication forever?

Even if the symptoms improved on the drugs, treating ADHD symptoms with medication for a lifetime leads to increased dosages of drugs with increased side-effects. A child diagnosed with the problem at age six will most likely be placed on medication. If the medication is effective in the short run, that child will continue on that medication as long as it is effective. When it becomes less effective, the dosage of the drug will be changed until a new, increased dosage is found to be effective or until another drug is tried or added.

What happens when the drug is not effective?

When one drug is not effective, often another is tried or added to the original regimen. Many of the children I see in my office have been offered other drug options by their previous physician. But many parents who come to see me are concerned with the constant trial of drugs, especially when the drugs become more and more potent and the side-effects more and more serious.

Are these drugs dangerous?

These drugs are very serious substances. I am really concerned by their frequent use in young children. Ritalin, used for many years for children with behavioral problems, is still a substance that is structurally like amphetamines. It is a controlled substance because the government has concerns that it can be abused. Dexedrine is also a controlled substance. As I explained, a controlled substance means that a government drug agent somewhere has a record of your child's Ritalin prescription on file. That's the law.

ABC's *20/20* show (October 27, 1995) revealed abuses, citing incidents in which children are snorting Ritalin, teachers and pharmacists are stealing it, and parents are selling it. Tim Benedick of the Ohio State Pharmacy Board said on the same *20/20* show that "It [Ritalin] is highly addictive. It is speed."[11]

Many of the children I have seen on Ritalin are often very subdued; others have had adverse reactions or a worsening of their symptoms. Parents report that their young children are like "zombies" on it. It can have very different effects on different individuals. Teenagers tell me and their parents that they don't like the way it makes them feel, and they don't want to take it.

Cocainelike substance

I call Ritalin "pediatric cocaine." The drug Ritalin, or its generic equivalent, methylphenidate HCl, is very similar to cocaine. Both drugs use the same receptor site in the brain, give the same "high," and in medical research are used interchangeably. The only difference appears to be that cocaine leaves the receptor site more quickly, possibly making it more addictive.[4] It is no surprise that we have a drug problem in this country when we prescribe drugs—that use the same receptor in the brain as cocaine—to children as young as three years of age. Are we teaching children that drugs are the answer to everything? I believe that is why Ritalin is being abused in the same manner that cocaine is abused. Ritalin is just legally prescribed; cocaine is not.

The side-effects

All drugs have side-effects. Ritalin has been used for many years, so we are very familiar with the short-term side-effects of that drug. The known short-term side-effects of Ritalin include loss of appetite, decreased growth, tics, visual disturbances, nervousness, insomnia, depression, social withdrawal, irritability, abdominal pain, increased heart rate, and psychoticlike symptoms.[10,15] Again, these are side-effects which occur from short-term use. Since long-term use is a relatively new phenomenon, the long-term side-effects have yet to be discovered. We don't yet know how the long-term use of Ritalin will affect our children's hearts, kidneys, or immune systems. In essence, the long-term studies are being conducted right now, on our children, without you or them even being aware of it. The drug companies make it clear in their drug insert that the safety and efficacy of the long-term use of Ritalin in children is not available.

The drug insert that comes with the medication reveals that the medication is not to be given unless environmental causes of the problem have been ruled out. And the drug insert advises that Ritalin should not be given without other concurrent treatments such as academic and behavioral modification.[15] Sometimes this drug insert is removed from the medication package. You can ask your pharmacist to include it whenever you get any prescription filled.

Who can take the drugs?

The drug insert that comes with the medication instructs that Ritalin is not to be given to children under the age of six since safety and efficacy for this age group has not been established.[15]

However, I hear daily about children under the age of six (even as young as three years of age) who have been prescribed this drug.

Are the drugs addictive?

There is not a good understanding of the mechanism by which Ritalin works on the behavior of children. According to the drug insert and the *Physicians' Desk Reference* (PDR) (which contains the same information about the drugs as the drug insert and can be obtained at the library or purchased at a bookstore), there is a possibility for a child to become psychologically dependent on the drug, and tolerance can develop.[15] This means that eventually there is the potential that a stronger dose would be needed to accomplish the same results. Kids have discovered that they can snort it and get a high, so it does appear to have the same properties as addictive drugs. Since it so closely resembles cocaine, I think we must consider it addictive.

Are there other drugs used to treat ADHD?

There are many other drugs that are prescribed to treat ADHD symptoms.

Dextroamphetamine (Dexedrine) has been a favorite in the past, but appears to have been used less frequently in recent years. It is an amphetamine, and also a controlled substance that has been sold as a street drug. Because of the side-effect of appetite suppression, it was used as a "diet" pill in the sixties, but found to have too high a potential for abuse to continue to be used for that purpose on a regular basis: While it appears to be too dangerous for adults to take on a regular basis, it is given freely and readily to children. It has side-effects similar to Ritalin.[5,8,10,15]

Pemoline (Cylert) is probably the next most frequently used drug. At least, it was for some time, until it was observed that there is a potential for liver damage with continued use. There have been rare cases of hepatic-related fatalities of patients taking Cylert. Cylert's only indication for use is for ADHD symptoms. It is a central nervous system stimulant, and has multiple side-effects.[5,8,10,15]

Imipramine hydrochloride (Tofranil) is a tricyclic antidepressant and another popular drug treatment for ADHD symptoms. This was one of the drugs used to treat my daughter's bladder infections and possibly contributed to her illness. Again, the mechanism of the drug is not really understood. While it has an indication for use as an antidepressant as well as for enuresis (bed-wetting) in children, it is not indicated for the treatment of ADHD. However, Tofranil is being used extensively for this purpose. Tofranil has not been approved for use in children under six years of age and is indicated for older children only for bed-wetting problems. According to the drug insert, this drug can cause bone marrow depression, as well as cardiac, neurological, endocrine, and GI problems. Though the manufacturer claims it is not addictive, withdrawal symptoms can occur after prolonged treatment and following abrupt withdrawal of the drug.[8,15]

Desipramine (Norpramin) is another antidepressant used for ADHD, but fortunately it is used less frequently than others. Norpramin's drug insert states that the drug should not be used in children at all. The drug is officially approved for the treatment of depression. Some doctors are now diagnosing children exhibiting ADHD-type symptoms as depressed. There have been cases of sudden cardiac death in children who were treated with Norpramin. Of course, this is a very rare occurrence.[8,15]

Antiseizure medications were also popular for a while for the treatment of ADHD. Children who had no evidence of seizures were being prescribed antiseizure drugs. Since that time, it has been determined that antiseizure medications are to be used only to treat patients with seizures.[15] In addition, the antiseizure drugs have been associated with creating learning disabilities.[14,15]

Clonidine (Catapres) is an adult antihypertensive drug. It has not been tested on children for the purpose of treating ADHD symptoms and is not indicated for anything but hypertension in adults.[9,15] The children I have seen on this drug often have a lower blood pressure and sleep constantly. I vividly recall one little girl who was taking clonidine. When her parents brought her to my office, we never saw her awake until she discontinued the clonidine.

Prozac is the latest major drug being used for the symptoms of ADHD, according to my patients in California. I have heard mention of its use in Texas, where I practice. With the news on ABC's *20/20* about Ritalin abuse, I predict that we will begin to see a lot more children on Prozac as an alternative to Ritalin.

What does it mean for a drug to be "indicated"?

"Indicated" means that the drugs have actually gone through testing to qualify for the use indicated. From the above list, only three drugs are indicated for use in treating ADHD: Ritalin, Dexedrine, and Cylert.[5,15] The others have been adopted for use without the rigorous testing that is required for a drug to become qualified as indicated.

If a drug is indicated for treating ADHD symptoms, does that mean it is safe to use on children?

Of the drugs indicated for treatment of ADHD, all have multiple and severe potential side-effects. Of course, most drugs carry potential side-effects. One must weigh the side-effects with the possible positive results and decide what is best to do. I have heard other doctors say there are no side-effects. That statement is simply not true.

If drugs make my child focus better, won't my child do better in school?

If the drug does work for a child, it probably won't make all of the problems go away. Even if it does make some of the problems go away, they will stay away only as long as the child is taking the drug. And the potential for side-effects remain as long as the child is taking the drug. Ritalin causes adults and children *without* ADHD symptoms to focus better, the same way it affects adults and children who actually *do* have ADHD symptoms.[6] If you give your child medication and the child improves, it doesn't mean the ADHD symptoms have gone away. It means that the drug is covering up the symptoms and the underlying problem. The drug companies and doctors have led us to believe that this is an appropriate way to deal with our medical problems. While sometimes we must treat symptoms with drugs, we must not stop looking for the underlying cause. A Comprehensive Review Article published in the 1990 issue of the *Journal of the American Academy of Child and Adolescent Psychiatry* found that the short-term impact of stimulants on children with ADHD included improved behavior, performance, and attention. However, there was little evidence that stimulants improved sustained attention, retention of information, anger control, or scholastic achievement.[6]

In fact, the study found that there was no difference between treated and untreated hyperactives in the number of grades failed or in achievement scores. While hyperactive children attended fewer junior colleges and universities and in high school failed more grades and dropped out more frequently, medicated children with ADHD symptoms did not differ from untreated children in these areas. In addition, studies of the immediate effects of stimulant medication have shown few significant positive effects on peer relations. "Comprehensive studies of long-lasting effects of stimulants show little support for the efficacy of drug use in treating children with ADHD symptoms."[6]

Drug-prescribing doctors

Everything doctors learn in medical school, except for the basic science courses, revolves around treating symptoms with drugs. Doctors learn all about the human body through such courses as anatomy, physiology, immunology, and biochemistry. Doctors then learn in pathology class how to diagnose, or name, a disease, and how to treat the symptoms, or prescribe drugs, in pharmacology class. From then on, during rotations, internships, and residencies, doctors learn more and more about treating diseases with drugs. This is what they are taught.

After medical school

At continuing medical education meetings, drug companies sponsor physicians' lectures. The lecturing doctor, who is usually paid an honorarium from the drug company, tells the audience of doctors about the drug he or she is now using as the "best current treatment" for various diseases. The drug of choice is, of course, manufactured by the sponsoring drug company.

At national medical meetings, the drug companies set up booths to display their drugs. I have seen huge convention centers filled with drug company booths, each one educating the doctors about the advantages of their standard and new drugs. They almost always give doctors specialty items such as pens and note pads and other incentives to stop by the booth. To an outside observer, it could easily look like an adult Halloween celebration, with the doctors going from booth to booth with bags, collecting "goodies" from the drug companies. But these goodies serve a very real purpose for the drug companies. They keep the name of the drugs in front of the doctors when they go back to their offices and use the free items. This makes it more likely that, when it is time to write prescriptions for their patients, they will remember that company's drug. And it works. This practice is straight out of a basic marketing course. But it also demonstrates how this drug dependency is reinforced and why drugs remain the standard first-line treatment. Physicians are simply not getting educated or informed about any other options. When doctors do hear about other treatment options, they usually don't listen, don't understand it, or don't believe it, because they have been so well taught to practice drug medicine. The nondrug options do not fit into their drug-treatment model, therefore they discount it. This is sad. Many of these physicians really believe that drug treatment is the only way or the best way. But it is mostly sad for the patients who are exposed to only drug-related medicine.

The making of a new drug

Some new drugs are basically not new. In fact they are based on either old standard drugs or natural compounds. These standard or natural drugs are inexpensive and readily available and cannot be patented or owned by a drug company. If they cannot be patented, the drug company cannot make as much money on them, so there is no incentive to manufacture them. So how can an American drug company carve out a new market and make a good profit in a capitalist economy? The company develops a new drug, of course. Never mind that there is already an inexpensive and effective drug available, often with minimal side-effects. Instead, a motivated drug company will take the chemical composition of these established drugs, change the chemical molecules ever so slightly and voila, a new drug is developed, one that can be owned and patented by the drug company.

After going through double-blind studies and the FDA approval process, the marketing begins. Physicians are "educated" about the advantages of this "new and better" drug through seminars, lectures, exhibits, medical journal ads, free items with the new drug's name stamped in full view and, of course, through the "drug rep," who brings samples of the new drug, gifts, and lunch to the doctor's office. After such a marketing campaign, how can the doctor even remember the other drugs or options available for his or her patients?

What happens when the patent on a drug runs out and any drug company can produce the generic version of this well-marketed drug? Drug companies have a new strategy. Now when the patent runs out, the drug goes "over the counter," and a whole new marketing campaign begins, directed at the consumer. Instead of marketing the drug to the doctor for prescribing, the drug company now has a whole new market . . . the patients. I am bewildered at how a prescription drug that had to be prescribed by a doctor while the drug was under a patent miraculously becomes safe for the patient to self-prescribe at exactly the same time the patent runs out. And why did it cost so much more when it was a prescription drug? Was it because there was no competition, and the public had no choice so the drug company could charge whatever the market would bear? Is it about money or is it about our health and safety?

Don't medical journals introduce doctors to nondrug therapies?

One would like to believe that the medical journals are unbiased and deliver significant new information to physicians. But page after page of the journals are covered with advertisements from drug manufacturers. If a journal wants to continue to be sponsored by the drug companies, they certainly don't put a lot of antidrug or alternative treatment articles in the magazines. Recently, I pulled at random a medical journal from a stack in my office. Sixty percent of the 230 pages in the journal were ads from pharmaceutical companies.

Wouldn't the medical journals print sound, proven studies about nondrug treatments?

It is almost impossible to get a research grant to establish the efficacy of any treatment other than a medication. The drug companies spend millions if not billions of dollars on research. Who else has the kind of money to spend on the research of alternative treatments? Even the National Institutes of Health, who began doing alternative medicine research a couple of years ago, gave only a token amount of money toward the funding of such research.

How are drugs tested?

The scientific method, which is considered the gold standard for any medical research, is, I believe, biased in favor of drugs. To put any treatment through the scientific method of proof, one must be able to establish that a double-blind study has been accomplished. A double-blind study means that a group of subjects is given a certain treatment, usually a medication, and a control group is given another treatment, called a placebo. A placebo is something that is expected to have no effect on the subject. Neither the subjects nor the physician knows which treatment is given to whom. The study is evaluated to see if the real treatment was any better than the placebo. Since the researcher and the subject do not know which treatment they are getting, the chance of personal bias influencing the results is presumed to be nonexistent.

But this is not always the case. One physician I know told me about a research project in which she participated at a major cancer center. The physicians peeked in the envelope to see if it contained a placebo or the actual drug being tested. The physicians then decided which patients would receive the drug and which would receive the placebo. They then gave their choice to the participants in the study. This is not how a double-blind study should be done. It does, however, show that not all studies, even double-blind ones, are necessarily accurate. Most of the drugs currently used for the treatment of ADHD symptoms have not gone through double-blind studies to show their effectiveness for this purpose. Yet they continue to be used for this purpose.

Can the scientific method for research be used to study nondrug treatments?

To do a double-blind study, one must be able to do something to the patient that can be kept secret from the patient and from the doctor. There are not many treatments other than drugs that can work in a double-blind format, but scientists have been literally brainwashed to believe that this method is the only way to substantiate anything useful in medicine. Since practically the only treatments that can really undergo or fit into the double-blind study model *are* medications, what is considered a "useful" treatment will be limited and biased toward drug treatments. It doesn't seem to matter that a physician uses a nondrug treatment to help the patient feel better or get well. If the method of treatment has not been through a double-blind study, the method is not acceptable in Western medicine. This is true even with treatments such as acupuncture, herbs, and homeopathy—treatments that have been used successfully for thousands of years in other parts of the world.

Some of the treatments I use in my office cannot be utilized in a double-blind study format. Osteopathic manipulation therapy (OMT) is a treatment in which a patient is diagnosed and treated through palpation (see Chapter 10). Although I suppose I could practice OMT in such a way that the patient didn't know what I was doing, it would be impossible for me not to know I was doing it. Thus, since OMT is not able to fall into the double-blind format, it is not accepted as a traditional and acceptable form of Western medicine, even though it is very effective for the patient. Anything that does not fall into a double-blind study format and that Western medicine will not accept will be discounted by the medical establishment. One hears such statements as "It hasn't been proven." Patients who don't understand the limits of the double-blind studies can be influenced by such statements from the medical community. The patient then discounts what could be an effective treatment for their problems. Patients deserve to have all information available in order to make personal health care choices. I certainly wish that had been the case for me when my daughter first became ill. I would never have chosen the dangerous drug therapy that was prescribed for my daughter's chronic urinary tract problem.

What about accepted methods of treatment like surgery? Do they fall into the double-blind format?

It is nearly impossible to perform surgery in a double-blind fashion. It would be considered unethical to perform surgery on someone, opening them up, not doing anything once they are opened, and then closing them back up so that the patient does not know if he actually had something repaired or not. And the doctor would certainly know if he actually performed a surgical procedure on the patient or just simply cut him open and closed him up. Yet new surgical techniques that have not been subjected to double-blind studies are accepted all the time. Someone comes up with a concept for a surgery, performs it, and never does a double-blind study. Interestingly, Western medical doctors accept new surgical treatments even though they have not been proven to be effective through double-blind studies but appear to be successful because of a positive outcome. There does seem to be a double standard when it comes to double-blind studies.

Hasn't the thinking about double-blind studies begun to shift?

Recently, there has been some interest in the importance of *outcome* studies and, hence, a bit less importance placed on

double-blind studies. The emphasis has not changed much, though. Occasionally an outcome study will be written up in the literature. There is even an "outcome journal" now. But remember that the editors of the journals have their own biases, and since they cannot publish every article that comes along, they must pick and choose the articles they print. Editors will most likely select articles that support their own beliefs and perhaps those of their advertisers.

For these reasons I am very skeptical about articles in medical journals. I expect the technique used and results found to be consistent with our basic knowledge of such areas as physiology and biochemistry. When the results go against common sense and basic knowledge, such as the research showing that sugar doesn't affect behavior, when it is a physiological fact that it certainly can and does in many individuals[16,19–22] (see Chapter 6 on low blood sugar), I have a lot of trouble accepting those articles at face value. As I covered in Chapter 2, I recognize that behind many of these studies are people trying to make money. Unfortunately, the patient's needs or best interests are not always at the top of the list of considerations.

The HMO model and managed care

Managed care is also about money. The current crisis in health care is not a result of a universal disillusionment about the conventional drug-treatment model of medicine. It is a result of the high cost of medicine. In my opinion, managed care is about managing cost more than managing care. We are just beginning to see news reports and Senate hearings about the problems resulting from managed care practices. Managed care patients have complained about being denied care, provided less effective treatments, and released from the hospital too quickly because care delivery, effective treatments, and longer hospital stays are not good for a company's bottom line. Is our care being rationed? Decisions about our health care are being made by unknown, non-medical business staff working at managed care companies, not by the patient and the physician. Managed care administrators and staff are awarded bonuses based on how much money they save their company—or, in other words, how much medical care the company does *not* have to provide. I believe people are motivated by personal incentives. Clearly, it appears that the incentive is in *not* providing you care if at all possible.

I attended a managed care seminar where I was told that we would have to practice medicine differently. Following is one of the examples the speaker used. If an older woman needs a hip replacement, the physician should try to delay the surgery by recommending the woman use a cane to help her walk. Due to her advanced age, she may not live long enough to have the surgery, thus helping keep the doctor's expenditures down and saving the company money. In fact, doctors who spend too much of the managed care company's money are called overutilizers. Overutilizers can be dropped from the managed care company's physician list.

Generally, it is cheaper to drug a patient's health problems. To get to the bottom of the problem will cost too much on the front end—unacceptable in a managed care environment. A narrow band of prescribed "cookie-cutter, one-size-fits-all" practices seems to be the standard of care under managed care rule. Such an approach can be painfully limited for patients whose health care may require more specific, individual services that fall outside the managed care service line.

That is why I do not participate in managed care. I do not want to practice under either the drug-oriented or the managed care model. My practice is based on finding the underlying cause of the problem and on the osteopathic philosophy (see Chapter 10). Most of my patients get better after treatment and have no need to return to my office. It would seem that if HMOs really wanted to save money in the long run without rationing health care and/or without jeopardizing the patient's health, they would look beyond their own money and drug-based models for the answers. After all, the most expensive kind of medicine is the kind that doesn't work. The public has to want more, expect more, demand more. Such changes are almost always consumer driven.

CHAPTER 4

WHAT ABOUT MENTAL HEALTH AND EDUCATIONAL SERVICES?

Mental health services and educational modifications, along with drugs, complete the triad as the standard of care for ADHD. Even the drug insert that accompanies a Ritalin prescription says that the drug is not to be used alone for ADHD symptoms. It is to be used in conjunction with environmental and educational modifications. But doctors most often prescribe only drugs for the symptoms.[2,3]

While mental health services and educational modifications are often overlooked as a part of the treatment for the symptoms of ADHD, I don't entirely agree with the way these services are being applied when they are used.

Psychiatric diagnosis?

As mentioned in Chapter 2, ADHD is considered to be a psychiatric diagnosis. This diagnosis is based on the symptoms in the DSM-IV. Since I believe the evaluation of those symptoms to be subjective, I question the validity of the diagnosis. It troubles me that parents are paying hundreds of dollars to have their children tested for ADHD when anyone who reads the list of symptoms in the DSM-IV could relate the symptoms to the boy or girl in question and decide if he or she qualified for the diagnosis. If he or she has attention problems in school but not at the evaluator's office, or had behavior problems at home but not at the evaluator's office, does that mean he or she does not have a problem? Of course not. A good evaluator will take the parents' and teacher's information into consideration. Remember that the evaluator you select to test your child may not have the same feelings about children's behavior as you do. If the therapist has high expectations of children, thinking they should sit still, listen, and obey no matter what the age or circumstances, that evaluator will have a different test result than one who thinks a child can talk, move around, and be creative. I once observed a psychologist "test" a young boy for ADHD. The psychologist became very upset when the child would not remain seated and listen to him, and in his anger was verbally abusive. He sat the child in a corner and pushed a table up in front of him so that the boy could not move. I seriously question the validity of the result of that "testing." The poor child was scared to death.

Psychological vs. physiological

Too much focus on the psychological side distracts us from looking for the real problem, which is often more physiological than psychological. Too often I have seen children who have had an expensive psychological evaluation without a proper medical workup. Since I think that such conditions as low blood sugar, allergies, and even thyroid dysfunction can contribute to ADHD symptoms and behavioral changes, the child should be medically evaluated and treated before jumping to the conclusion the problem is only psychological. But this appears to be done rarely. Last year I diagnosed four children with hyperthyroidism in four months. All of the children had been diagnosed as ADHD. When the thyroid problem was addressed, the symptoms (which had been called ADHD) resolved. How sad it is to see children drugged while their underlying health problems go untreated. No wonder symptoms return when the drug is discontinued.

Behavior

While I do not use ADHD as a diagnosis, I do think it is important to discuss behavior. If the child's behavior is interfering with his or her life at home or school, you have a problem. But the behavior is merely a symptom of something wrong with the child, medically or emotionally. Such behavior could indicate a problem with the situation in which the child has been placed.

In one case, a child was very good at home but was the problem student at school—disrupting the class on a regular basis. The teacher thought the child had ADHD. On a closer look, through a complete history of the boy's home environment, it was discovered that the father was very strict, requiring his son to be quiet and perfectly behaved at all times. For this child, the only place to let down was at school. A prescription of Ritalin would be inappropriate for him. A child cannot be perfect all day. Think about constantly carrying a 100-pound weight. Though you might be able to pick up the 100-pound weight, you cannot carry it around all day without putting it down. The same is true of children's behavior. Even if they can control themselves part of the time, eventually they must let down. Then you see what may be considered inappropriate behavior, if they let down at an inappropriate time and place.

Also, what is appropriate in one home may be considered inappropriate in another. As my children were growing up, I allowed them to play freely in the house, often being noisy and playing with toys in every room. In someone else's home, such actions have been construed as overly loud and making a mess. Such behavior would not be allowed. Whatever your rules are, if your child is unable to follow them, there is a problem. Something must change—either your expectations or your child's behavior. Labeling a child as ADHD does not fix the problem.

Psychologists are beneficial, too

The field of psychology should not be ignored. Every thought in our head affects how we feel and vice versa. The chemicals released in our bodies make our body function. These chemicals are neurological as well as immunological. The two systems are interconnected.

A doctor must consider what is going on in a child's life, physically, mentally, and emotionally. If a child is being abused, he or she certainly will not be able to concentrate in school. And behavioral changes can occur as a result of the abuse.

While I do not think that psychological problems are the underlying cause of the ADHD symptoms in most cases, I do think these children should be evaluated psychologically. Many times the emotional component is a result of another problem.

I also think psychologists and counselors can be important to helping a child get well. But psychologists are not physicians and are not always aware of the medical diagnosis and other treatment options for these symptoms. There are many modalities available through psychology that are beneficial. I refer often to therapists for hypnosis, biofeedback, relaxation, and counseling.

Behavioral modification

I have found that behavior modification is not helpful when a child is reacting to a health problem. Children cannot control themselves no matter how much behavioral modification they receive if their blood sugar has dropped, if their thyroid is over-active, or, as Dr. Doris Rapp says, "if they are reacting to something they touched, smelled, or ate." When they are not reacting to these things, behavioral modification is not necessary because the child is able to behave. A child who can control himself will do so. I believe all children want to please and succeed. When they are unable to do so, it is because they do not have control or they do not know or understand what is expected of them. So if they are reacting, behavioral modification won't help, and if they are not reacting, behavioral modification isn't necessary.

I believe the real reason to see a therapist for an evaluation is not to be tested for ADHD symptoms, but to be evaluated for other potential problems that could appear as ADHD symptoms. This is the same reason your child should have a thorough physical evaluation as well.

Potential problems that may cause ADHD-type symptoms and can be evaluated by a therapist include learning disabilities or learning differences, emotional problems, child abuse, or even lack of, or inappropriate, discipline. But I believe more often than not that ADHD symptoms have an underlying physical and/or educational cause rather than being mental or emotional. It is my opinion that children diagnosed with ADHD can have emotional and self-esteem problems as a result of being labeled ADHD.

Medical condition?

I do not believe ADHD is truly a medical condition. The only thing that makes ADHD a medical condition is that currently there is a drug used to treat it, and doctors tend to diagnose it. I do find that there is usually a medical condition that is causing the symptoms.

Many children these days are being diagnosed with depression in relationship to ADHD symptoms. Many of these children do appear depressed, but I am not convinced that the depression is the cause of the ADHD, but rather the symptoms of depression are a result of the ADHD symptoms. Another scenario would be that the ADHD symptoms and the depression both stem from the same underlying cause. Certainly if you go through life hearing "a different drummer" and being told that you are different, it will affect the way you feel about yourself and the way you feel physically. But it bothers me that the medical and psychological communities are trying to pin the etiology of ADHD symptoms on depression. I see many children in my practice who are on antidepressant medications for their ADHD symptoms. Since the antidepressant drugs are not intended for use for ADHD symptoms, I wonder if the medical community is labeling children whose symptoms improve on antidepressant drugs as being depressed, using the depression diagnosis as another label so that doctors can more comfortably prescribe the antidepressant drug for use as indicated.

One doctor I heard speak said that he thought most, if not all, ADHD was actually depression. He stated that he thinks that everyone who has ADHD symptoms should be on antidepressant drugs or the drug lithium for manic-depression or bipolar disorder. Though I do not like the ADHD label given to children, I believe it is more benign than one of manic-depression or bipolar.

Too often the drugs prescribed are not effective and another drug must be tried. I had one child in my office who was taking four different drugs at the same time for his behavior. When that combination didn't work, he was placed on four other drugs. The second combination did not benefit him, either. When I asked his mother if the drugs were working, she said, "No, we wouldn't be here if they were working. You stop looking for answers when you get results." Her child was on several different types of serious medications without relief. As long as the doctor thinks that drugs are the only solution, he will use more drugs and different drugs to treat a condition. There is a saying that "If all you have is a hammer, everything looks like a nail." The same is true with ADHD. If all you have is a prescription pad, everyone gets a drug.

Learning differences

Problems due to learning differences are other reasons to have your child evaluated. Testing for learning disabilities is an objective process that can help point out the source of the learning problem. A learning disability (or a learning difference, as I prefer to call it), can affect a child emotionally. Difficulty learning can make a child feel different from others and may lead to the symptoms of depression. But giving the child an antidepressant medication will only cover up the symptoms, not make the problem go away. The learning difference should be addressed. The child then might not need drugs. (See Chapter 8 on learning differences.)

While we teach our children how to read, add, subtract, multiply, and divide, we usually assume that they automatically know how to learn, that learning is an inherent ability, one that doesn't need to be taught. We assume that everyone knows how to learn and if they don't learn, they are disabled. This is inappropriate. We must teach our children how to learn just as we teach them how to read.

There are some who seem to be born with the ability to learn, and they certainly have an advantage. There are also children who begin reading on their own, and others who must be taught to read. My son appeared to be born with the ability to do math. At the age of four he could multiply two-digit numbers in his head—no one taught him how to do that. At the same age he also computed square roots aloud while buckled into the backseat of our car on the way to preschool. No one taught him how to do that, either. Some children need to be taught how to read or do math; others don't. Some need to be taught how to learn, and others don't.

Of course everyone can learn *some* things. What comes naturally in learning is very individualized. Some can draw or paint without instruction. Others can sit down and play the piano with no music lessons. We call this a gift, and it certainly is. But we also know that someone without this gift can, with the proper instruction and with time and practice, learn to play the piano. It may take them months or even years to become accomplished, but we don't call them learning disabled because they cannot sit down and play like gifted children do. No, we give them the time to practice, and we take the time to teach them. Many children diagnosed with ADHD or learning disabilities have similar situations. They often have gifts, perhaps creative endeavors that they can do naturally well, but they also have areas, such as math or reading, in which they struggle.

We must stop calling these children learning disabled. The term "learning differences" is used in some places, and I support its use. These children are not learning disabled. In fact, they are often very bright and especially gifted in some area outside of school. It is our responsibility to teach children how to learn. We must not assume they are disabled because they cannot learn without instruction.

"Learning disabled," just like ADHD, is a label—nothing more. It is useless in addressing the underlying cause of the problem. Learning disabilities can be evaluated. If a child has a problem learning in school, we must know the source of the problem, what area of learning is problematic for him or her, and address that problem. A child with a learning difference may be erroneously labeled ADHD. (See Chapter 8.)

Expecting too much

We put incredible pressures on children at such young ages that we often forget how a child is supposed to behave. Children spend much of their time in places away from home, with teachers paid to supervise them. The teachers' jobs are much easier if all of the children are perfectly well behaved and give them no trouble. But is there really anything wrong with a three-year-old child who cannot sit quietly all day, who speaks out of turn, becomes frustrated and who hits other children occasionally? No, there isn't. These behaviors have been going on for centuries, and most are normal.

SECTION II

HOW I TREAT
ADHD
WITHOUT DRUGS

CHAPTER 5

A PHYSICIAN'S APPROACH

A symptom is simply the body's way of letting you know that something is wrong. It is a clue, a red flag. The symptom should not be covered over by a drug. Doing so will keep you from finding out what the body is trying to tell you—what's really wrong. So it is with ADHD symptoms. They are also the body's way of saying something is wrong.

In fact, I have found that children with ADHD symptoms usually do have an underlying health problem that has gone undiagnosed and untreated. This is a common observation in my office. It simply doesn't make sense that the medical establishment would choose to drug these children so quickly without investigating all possibilities. We should expect more from medicine.

A medical school professor of mine, Dr. Irvin Korr, once said that "the body is not sick because it has a disease, but instead the body has a disease because it is sick." It makes sense, then, to say that a child is not sick because the child has the symptoms called ADHD, but rather the child has the symptoms called ADHD because there is something wrong with the child. And we need to find out what is wrong, and treat it so the symptoms can go away.

If you have an occasional headache and aspirin or aceta-minophen (Tylenol) relieves the symptoms, then occasionally treating the symptoms is fine. But if you have a headache every day and cover up the symptoms every day with a stronger and stronger drug, you may never find out the cause of your headaches. The headaches could be caused by stress, by allergies, or even by a tumor. If you have them every day, wouldn't you want to know what was wrong so you could stop having headaches altogether and remove any potential risk of the chronic use of a drug?

My approach to health care is based on three things: (1) the osteopathic philosophy; (2) our current scientific knowledge of how the body works physiologically, and (3) common sense. There is no physiological basis for the diagnosis of ADHD. So it doesn't make sense to name it. If we give it a name and then drug it, it can very well stop us from looking for the real cause. The osteo-pathic philosophy states that the body has an inherent ability to heal itself if the impediments to good health are removed. Guided by this philosophy, I will look at the symptoms of ADHD as clues that there is an imbalance within the body or a negative influence from outside the body. Using those clues, I will look for and treat that underlying problem instead of drugging the symptoms.

If you stepped on a nail and the nail became embedded in your foot and caused an infection, you would expect the doctor to re-move the nail. You would not expect the doctor to examine the extent of redness and the swelling of the foot, test the infected tissue for the exact type of infection occurring on the foot, clean the area, bandage it, and send you home with a prescription for antibiotics and orders to stay off the foot until it is healed, leav-ing the embedded nail in your foot. Imagine—the infection keeps recurring because the source of the problem is still embedded in your body. The doctor simply prescribes stronger and stronger antibiotics to control the infection. And when that doesn't solve the infection problem, the doctor puts you on a long-term antibiotic treatment and declares you to be handicapped with a chronic infection that prevents you from walking on your foot. You cannot play sports or engage in other outside activities. In addition, you are exposed to the side-effects of long-term antibiotic drug use, and the underlying problem of the nail in your foot will still be there when they take you off the medication.

This, in my opinion, is what we are doing to our children labeled with ADHD. It doesn't make sense to put young children on such serious drugs for long periods of time when these drugs do no more than cover up symptoms. We must look for and treat the underlying cause of the symptoms.

Some practitioners may tell parents that the underlying causes of ADHD symptoms are not known. I disagree most strenuously. In my practice, I have had a great deal of success treating these children by looking for the underlying problem and by treating that, rather than merely applying drugs to control a child's symptoms. Subsequent chapters deal with each of these potential underlying causes separately.

What are the most common underlying causes of the symptoms called ADHD?

The most common underlying causes I find in my practice include:

- Hypoglycemia or low blood sugar level (Chapter 6)
- Allergies (Chapter 7)
- Learning disabilities (Chapter 8)
- Hyperthyroidism (Chapter 9)
- Dietary factors (Chapter 9)

I developed my own approach to the practice of medicine as a direct result of what happened to my own child and my frightening experiences with the doctors who treated her. My approach is based on the osteopathic philosophy (see Chapter 10), which supports the practice of looking for the underlying cause and assisting the body's ability to heal itself. My approach is also based on the approach used by my mentor, Dr. Gary Campbell, and other fine physicians whom I have had the opportunity to learn from and work with since I went to medical school. Ironically, they are not all DOs (osteopathic physicians). Many are MDs who have developed and practice a similar philosophy

In medical school, I awakened to the real, and many times hidden, limitations of medicine. Medicine is not an exact science. It is not always applied in a sensible or rational manner by those practicing. When you see medicine for what it is, it can profoundly change your opinion and trust of medicine. You can become cynical or productive. I believe it did both for me. Cynical, because I am continually reminded of the problems in medicine, and productive because I am determined to practice differently. On a daily basis patients come to my office as frustrated, wounded, and scared as I once was when I was looking for help for my daughter. The doctors they have seen prior to me prescribed drug after drug after drug without successful results. These patients want something else, something better, something that works. They know their child deserves that.

If at first you don't succeed—use fear tactics

A parent expressed concerns about a nutrient, magnesium, which I had prescribed for her child. When she asked another doctor about it, he told her magnesium was dangerous. Now there is absolutely nothing dangerous about this treatment at the dose I recommended. It is a natural substance, a mineral that is found in the body naturally. In fact, if the human body does not have enough magnesium, the body won't work properly. But this other doctor used what I call fear tactics on this parent. If he had known anything at all about magnesium, he would not have said these things. But apparently he did not know anything about it.

Doctors usually learn little about nutrition in medical school. As already discussed, they learn a lot about drugs. It would have been more appropriate for the other doctor simply to tell the mother that he did not know anything about magnesium. But there are a couple of things accomplished when the doctor tells the parent that a nutrient is dangerous. He thinks it will make him appear less ignorant. Doctors never seem to want to admit when they don't know something. I remember one physician in my medical training. He expected you to know everything in your head. You weren't allowed to look up anything. This, of course, was absurd. No doctor should rely only on what he can remember. The amount of medical information today is staggering. If you limit yourself to what you can remember in your own head, you wouldn't be a very good doctor. But that kind of attitude has a way of perpetuating itself. If medical students think that they have to know everything (and if they don't, they will be considered stupid by the doctor teaching them), then they are always going to try to hide their ignorance. They then continue that behavior with their patients.

The other thing the doctor accomplished by saying the nutrient wasn't safe was trying to make his colleague look bad. In today's medical marketplace, the competition is stiff. No doctor wants to lose a patient, so if the other doctor can say that the prescription a competitor is writing is dangerous, he might keep the patient (but he rarely does).

I always tell patients not to trust me, but to get information from me and others, and then make decisions based on what makes sense to them. For example, the patient mentioned earlier asked the doctor to explain why the magnesium I had recommended was dangerous. I had given her many articles to read about magnesium, which explained its use and safety. She gave the other doctor the articles and asked him to explain his position in light of the information she had, but he would not. He could not tell her why he thought the nutrient was dangerous, yet I could show her through documentation and scientific studies why the nutrient was safe. I told her that she should not use anything with which she wasn't completely comfortable. She took all of the information and read it and educated herself, and tried to get the other doctor to explain why he thought it was dangerous. Since he would not, she decided to give her child the nutrient. It helped.

Drug therapy

The way medicine is taught and learned in medical school is based on drugs. Because of this, doctors do not know of other modalities of treatment. Drug therapy was truly a lifesaver in the early part of this century when bacterial epidemics were prevalent.

But today the medical problems are very different. We are plagued with chronic health problems that are life-style based. And they will not go away unless we change that life-style. Covering up the symptoms with a drug doesn't really help. We know that we can treat hypertension with a drug and lower the blood pressure. But it doesn't cure the problem. If you stop the drug, the blood pressure will go right back up. So even though we may need to use drugs to treat symptoms at times, we should remember that all we are doing is treating the symptoms. If the person is going to get well and stay well, we are going to have to figure out what the underlying cause of the problem is. Then there will have to be some life-style changes.

The symptoms of ADHD are not a result of a drug deficiency, though I have heard a number of doctors refer to it as being a Ritalin deficiency. Dr. A. T. Still, the founder of osteopathy, used to say that "Man should study and use the drugs compounded in his own body."[18] If there is a receptor in the body for Ritalin and cocaine, then there must be a chemical in the body that is using the same receptor. Surely, Mother Nature did not put a receptor site in the brain on the chance that these drugs would eventually be manufactured. We must figure out why the body isn't using the natural chemical, the one that is already in the body. And we must figure out what needs to be done so that the body can produce or more effectively use that natural chemical. If the body is working as it was intended, it wouldn't need any additional drugs to work properly.

Doctors seem to have a lot of trouble with this concept. I remember one doctor telling me, in a discussion about a natural remedy, that if the herb really was beneficial, then we needed to figure out what chemical in the herb was causing the benefit and make a drug out of it. This seemed quite absurd to me. Why not just take the natural herb? But he had been taught to think that everything must be treated with a drug, and he could not get beyond that mind set.

The mountain of health

The body is filled with numerous chemicals that help it work properly. In addition to the essential chemicals that occur naturally in the body, there are other essential chemicals that must be obtained from our diet. Without both kinds, we cannot function properly. While some drugs are based on these natural chemicals and are used to replace them in our body (for example, insulin for diabetics), other replacement drugs do not at all resemble the natural chemicals in our body.

Vitamins, minerals, and other nutrients that we obtain from our diet are necessary as enzymes and cofactors in biochemical reactions. The concept that we get all the nutrients we need from a balanced diet is no longer valid. The typical American diet does not usually represent a good balanced diet. In addition, our body's need for nutrients is increasing as we deal with the increased pollution, stress, chemicals, and allergens in our environment.

I developed a concept that I call the Mountain of Health that will illustrate these points and help shed some light on the reason why many people who do not feel healthy are still not considered ill. I first referred to the Mountain of Health in the *Healthy School Handbook*, which was published by the National Education Association.[17]

Ideally, when we start out in life, we're at the top of this mountain enjoying optimum health. Unfortunately, there are things that can happen that cause us to slide down the mountain some, even before we are born. But ideally we started out at the top of the mountain at conception. During our lifetime, various insults and injuries to our bodies cause us to gradually or sometimes rapidly slide down the mountain until we finally fall off the Mountain of Health and land in the Valley of Disease. Sometimes we climb back out, and sometimes we do not. Poor diet, pollutants, stress, allergens, inactivity, and chemical exposures can push us farther down the mountain. In general our bodies can defend and repair themselves against these various insults. But if we suffer too many insults, they can overwhelm our bodies' immune systems, and we begin to break down physically. With the physical breakdown, we can become concerned, depressed, or angry about how we feel. This emotional component can add another insult to the body, pushing us even farther down the Mountain of Health, ever closer to the brink.

Many of us sit right on the brink of disease most of our lifetime, a place where one assault can knock us off the cliff and into the Valley of Disease. We might take a medication that covers up symptoms, that helps us crawl back up where we sit precariously perched on the brink once again, until something else comes along and knocks us off. We can sit there, passively hoping that we won't be knocked off again, or we can decide that we want to turn around our lives and work our way back up this Mountain of Health. With a higher position on the mountain, we will be stronger and more prepared to handle the next insult that comes our way.

Why do some people get sick when exposed to a virus or bacterium, and others do not?

The Mountain of Health explains why only some people get sick when everyone in a room gets exposed to a virus. Imagine two hundred people on board an airplane, and one passenger has a virus. During flight, the air is recirculated throughout the cabin. When the passengers reach their destination, 25 percent of them are sick from that virus. But the rest of the people are fine. That may be because each passenger was sitting at a different place on the Mountain of Health. The people sitting on the brink had no reserve with which to fight the virus, so they were the ones who were most likely to become ill from the virus, falling into the Valley of Disease.

It has been documented that stress can lower our immune system and leave us more susceptible to colds and flu. There is emotional stress and there is physical stress. When our bodies are constantly fighting off chronic physical problems, we are constantly under physical stress. Other people, not affected by chronic health problems, may be farther up the mountain and less susceptible to the virus. While exposure to the virus may have caused them to slide down the mountain a little bit, their immune system had enough energy and reserve to fight off the virus successfully, and they were able to move right back up to their prior position on the mountain. That's because their bodies' immune systems were not overwhelmed and could work well to fend off the virus. Emotional stress can affect our immune system in the same way.

Good health

I do not believe that good health is simply the absence of disease. To me, good health means that the body is working optimally in its most natural state. That is what places people at the top of the mountain.

We often think of the elderly as not being very healthy because they've had to endure years of insults to their bodies. But young children can also be at the bottom of the mountain, teetering on the brink of disease—even very early in life. This has been the case with many of the children I see who have been diagnosed with ADHD. When we remove the most troubling irritants to their bodies and help build up their immune systems, we see dramatic improvement and even elimination of their symptoms.

When a child comes to my office with symptoms of ADHD,

I find it is because something has caused that child to slide down the Mountain of Health. Giving a child a drug to cover the symptom will not help the child back up the mountain. It will not help the child's body work optimally in its most natural state. In fact these drugs will interfere with the natural function of the body. That is why I look for and treat the underlying cause.

Years ago when we thought children outgrew the symptoms of ADHD, it was probably all right to treat them temporarily for the symptoms. If they outgrew the symptoms, the drug could be stopped. But today we know better. We know that they do not outgrow the symptoms and must stay on drugs forever if the problem is not corrected. This is why the medical attitude must change. These children are not growing out of the problem, and the drugs don't even help with all of the symptoms. We cannot leave these children on these kinds of drugs for life. We don't even know what the long-term side-effects might be. And the drugs do not fix the problem. This is such a major change in thought process for doctors. Anything that appears to be different from their own medical model is poorly tolerated. Since they know nothing about these other ways to treat, many feel they must say such alternatives are wrong. These other ways are not wrong, but are based on the basic elements and concepts of physiology, anatomy, biochemistry, and immunology. And they are based on the recognition that we do not yet know everything there is to know in medicine. The only way to learn, understand, and improve is to keep an open mind.

Finding and fixing the underlying cause

Looking for the underlying cause of a problem will often lead to nutrition since nutrition underlies every way the body works.

The body cannot function properly without the right nutrients. Looking for the underlying cause takes a knowledge and understanding of how the body works, beyond obvious symptoms.

Finding the underlying cause of a problem and fixing it is the only way to achieve long-term results. Jason, the boy in the second chapter, would not have gotten well and been able to accomplish all that he has accomplished if we had not found and treated his hypoglycemia, the underlying problem.

Today, parents of children who are diagnosed with ADHD are told that drugs are the only treatment. This is because the only treatment their doctor knows about is drug treatment. This does not mean there is no other way. These children are often prescribed drugs with very serious side-effects. Such drugs, when effective, treat only the symptoms and do nothing for the underlying problem. Many of these parents report that their physicians do not listen to the parents' observations about their own child. One parent told me that she was still giving her child sugar even though she had observed that sugar definitely changed his behavior for the worse. When I asked why she still allowed him to have sugar, she said that her pediatrician had told her that sugar does not affect behavior. Therefore, she decided her observations of her own child must be wrong. She was denying her own experience, her own common sense, in deference to someone else's opinion, someone she had put in an authoritative position. Removing sugar from a child's diet is quite easy, safe, and very cost effective. It would have been so much easier and more productive to listen to her own good sense.

Having been in the position of both parent and patient with vital information to share, I know all too well how it feels to be discounted and ignored by physicians. Today, I work *with* my patients and listen to them. They know their child better than I do, better than anyone else does. I believe we must work together to find and fix the underlying cause of their child's symptoms of ADHD.

CHAPTER 6

HYPOGLYCEMIA/ LOW BLOOD SUGAR

TIM'S STORY

Tim came to my office at age sixteen. His symptoms were severe aggression and an agitated state. He constantly lost his temper and showed no control over his behavior. Tim was destructive, mean, angry, and often got into trouble with the law. But there were times when Tim was sweet and cooperative. The family never knew when he would become agitated and the sweet times were not often enough. His mother said that Tim could no longer acquire psychiatric insurance coverage as he had been in and out of psychiatric hospitals most of his short life without being helped for his problems. In addition, the family had spent more than $100,000 out of pocket for his care. Tim's mother brought him to my office as a last resort. Since I refuse to label patients and instead try to find the underlying causes of problems, I did some lab work. The lab work revealed that Tim had a severe case of hypoglycemia, or low blood sugar.

Easy to identify

Low blood sugar, or hypoglycemia, is the most significant underlying problem I find in children who exhibit behavioral problems. The symptoms of hypoglycemia are usually easy to iden-tify. The child who is agitated or irritable when he or she wakes up in the morning or before meals and then is better after eating is probably affected by hypoglycemia. The child with the Jekyll and Hyde behavior, who is sweet and fine one minute and then for no apparent reason is agitated, angry, and irritable the next, may have hypoglycemia.

Understanding the problem

When we look at physiology, we easily understand how low blood sugar can affect behavior. Without glucose (sugar) in the brain, people become unconscious or lapse into a coma. Nature has provided us with a backup system. When there is too little glucose in the bloodstream, and the brain would not have enough glucose available to work properly, the body releases a chemical to send more sugar into the bloodstream and to the brain, pre-venting a coma. The chemical released by our body to raise our blood sugar level back to normal is called epinephrine or adren-aline. But the chemical epinephrine has its own effect on the body.

Adrenaline: our "fight-or-flight" hormone

Epinephrine, commonly known as adrenaline, is a very im-portant chemical in our body, working on both the nervous sys-tem and the immune system. It affects our hearts, our lungs, our stomach, and our brain. Just about everything in our body is af-fected by adrenaline.

Adrenaline is often referred to as the "fight-or-flight" hor-mone. This is because it is a very protective hormone. The re-lease of adrenaline, which happens when we are scared or feel we are in danger, causes changes in our body that allow us to protect ourselves. The results include taking energy away from digestion and allowing a person to use the energy surge to run, fight, or otherwise protect himself from the perceived danger.

When adrenaline is dumped into a child's bloodstream, the child feels the fight-or-flight energy surge, reacting to the way the chemical makes him feel. Even if he is sitting comfortably in the classroom, trying to pay attention, an adrenaline release will have a profound effect. The pupils in the eyes dilate, the heart rate increases, and he cannot sit still. He cannot concentrate and can become agitated. Any little thing will now trigger him to act aggressively, even angrily. Such behavior is not conscious; the child does not choose to act that way. It is a physiological reaction. How uncomfortable and confusing to the mind and body to have to deal with common, day-to-day issues as if they were major, cataclysmic events. Yet adrenaline release occurs out of a natural protective mechanism, activated not by danger or fear but by other factors: what we eat or don't eat. Our bodies and chemicals within them react to the stimulation of our current dietary habits. The adrenaline causes the agitation, irritability, and shakiness that one may feel when hungry.

How do we get low blood sugar?

Hypoglycemia or low blood sugar occurs when our bloodstream does not have an adequate amount of sugar in it. This can occur in at least two different ways. One way is not to eat frequently enough. All of our foods eventually break down and convert to sugar, or glucose, in the body. If we don't eat frequently enough, there is not a continuous supply of sugar going into the bloodstream.

The second way to get low blood sugar is to eat sugar or foods high in sugar content. This may appear paradoxical. It would seem that if you ate sugar it would cause more sugar to go into the bloodstream, not less. However, some people have "reactive hypoglycemia." Reactive hypoglycemia can occur after ingesting refined carbohydrates, foods high in sugar, or alcohol. A person who has reactive hypoglycemia may have a metabolism problem, and the symptoms of low blood sugar may occur at a blood glucose level that is considered normal.

Foods that are high in sugar may cause an increase in insulin release from the pancreas. When insulin secretion was evaluated in one study, 90 percent of the patients with reactive hypoglycemia had insulin secretion abnormalities. If the adrenaline-type symptoms occur after the ingestion of refined carbohydrates, the diagnosis of reactive hypoglycemia can be made. The treatment is simply to remove the refined carbohydrates from the diet.[20]

If you eat a lot of refined carbohydrates, the sugar goes into your bloodstream very quickly. Although you may read and hear from your pediatrician that sugar does not affect behavior, I think most teachers (and probably most parents) who see the effects of sugar on children would say otherwise. Observing children at Halloween is a good example.

A study conducted at Yale University looked into this situation. Researchers fed a certain amount of sugar to adults and children. The sugar was an equivalent amount in the adults and children as a percentage of body weight. Blood glucose levels and blood adrenaline levels were measured every half hour for five hours. The blood sugar levels remained in the normal range in both adults and children, indicating that the adrenaline was doing its job keeping the glucose levels normal. However, the adrenaline levels in the children were ten times higher than normal up to five hours after ingesting the sugar. *All* of the children in the study had symptoms of increased adrenaline, while only one of the adults did. So it appears that sugar has a stronger effect on children.[16] Remember, these were "normal" children in this study. I believe that the so-called ADHD child would have an even more profound reaction.

There have been many medical research studies conducted on the link or nonlink between sugar and behavior. There may be a lack of understanding as to what is being studied. If one looks at basic physiology, it is hard to prove that sugar does *not* affect behavior. Eating sugar or foods containing a lot of sugar results in high sugar levels in the blood. The body then releases insulin to take the sugar or glucose to our cells. If too much glucose is taken from the blood, leaving too little glucose in the bloodstream, it is called hypoglycemia or low blood sugar. When the body becomes hypoglycemic, the chemical adrenaline is then released, causing the symptoms we have already discussed. In the Yale study, the authors concluded that children will release adrenaline with a higher glucose level in their bloodstream than adults.

Though many medical studies have implied there is no relationship between sugar and behavior, I take issue with the findings.[19,23] There are too many inconsistent factors. Several studies used two different kinds of sugars.[19] Sucrose sugar can evoke the insulin/adrenaline response (creating behavior problems) whereas fructose will not. To me, using two different types of sugar flaws the study and makes it invalid. Other issues to be considered in these studies would be whether or not sugars were given on an empty stomach or after a full meal. This can vary the absorption rate and alter the behavioral response as well as affect the consistency of the study. Another variable that can skew results is if a child is sensitive to any other ingredient in foods used in the study. Such sensitivity could cause a response similar to hypoglycemia and would be important relative to the accuracy of the study.

Symptoms of Hypoglycemia

High birth weight	Headaches
Sleeplessness	Moody
Temper tantrums	Can't sit still
Crying for no apparent reason	Craves sweets
Hyperactive/overactive	Shaky/irritable before meals
Uncontrollable	Behavior improved after meals
Angry/hostile	Agitated
Distractible	Defiant
Jekyll/Hyde behavior	

Other factors

Factors besides eating sugar that can cause low blood sugar levels include not eating frequently enough and food sensitivities. Often I will see a child in my office who does not eat breakfast. Sometimes he doesn't eat lunch, either. His behavior reflects the fact that he has not eaten. He gets low blood sugar followed by a release of adrenaline. It should come as no surprise that these children are no fun to be around. They are irritable, agitated, and ornery.

As for the food sensitivity reaction, which I cover in detail in the next chapter, there appears to be a relationship between the release of histamine (from an allergic reaction) and blood sugar levels.[24,25] This may be more of a neurological response than an immune system response. Though it is known that the response and effect is there, we need more research to determine exact mechanisms.

I was taught in medical school that premature and low-birth-weight babies would be more likely to have problems later in life. It came as quite a surprise when, in my first year of practice, I found that children who came into my office with the symptoms of ADHD had, for the most part, been high-birth-weight babies—most greater than seven and a half pounds. Many of them were in the eight-, nine-, and even ten-pound weight category. I have a theory that the greater birth weight may have something to do with the inability to process glucose properly, since big babies are often an indicator of a glucose-processing problem in the mother.

Fixing the problem

It is not necessary to do a glucose tolerance test on these children to diagnose hypoglycemia. If the child has the clinical symptoms—shaky and irritable when hungry, Jekyll/Hyde behaviors, calms down when fed—the clinical diagnosis can be made. The treatment for hypoglycemia is simple. Change the child's diet. Make sure that the child never gets hungry and eliminate refined carbohydrates, such as candy, cakes, pies, and soft drinks, from the child's diet, and determine foods to which the child is sensitive. (See Chapter 7 on allergy.)

I recommend that the child with symptoms of hypoglycemia eat several small meals each day. They should eat a breakfast that contains some protein (e.g., eggs, meat, sausage), and not eat sugary cereals or put sugar on their cereal. Syrup on pancakes or waffles likewise would not be a good idea. Nonsweetened jams and jellies make a good substitute for syrup. (Remember that children do not have to eat "breakfast" foods for breakfast. If you have leftovers from dinner the night before, they could have that. Sandwiches are fine, too.) A snack should be sent with them to school. I will write a prescription giving instructions for my patients to be allowed to eat a midmorning and midafternoon snack at school. If there is more than two hours between dinner and bedtime, another snack would be appropriate. It is best that the child with the symptoms of hypoglycemia go no longer than two hours without eating. If your child has this problem and tells you she is hungry, but dinner will be ready in thirty minutes, it is tempting to have her wait for dinner. I strongly suggest that you find something for your child to eat right then. Don't make her wait for dinner. When children with hypoglycemia get hungry, they need to eat now! Nut butter sandwiches (peanut butter, almond butter, etc.) without added sugar are good options for snacks because they are high in protein, fat, and complex carbohydrates. Trail mix snacks are good, too, because they contain nuts, seeds, and dried fruit. This type of food will break down slowly in the body and help to keep the blood sugar levels stable. With the blood sugar level stable, the body will not have to release adrenaline to correct the problem.

If children with hypoglycemia do not have adrenaline soaring through their bloodstream at inappropriate times, they can then control their behavior and will no longer exhibit behavioral symptoms. As a result, drugs will be unnecessary to treat the symptoms. It is much easier to correct this kind of problem at age six than at age seventeen.

TIM'S STORY: CONCLUSION

Hypoglycemia is often overlooked. Even the specialist who subsequently saw Tim discounted hypoglycemia, calling it irrelevant. But hypoglycemia can be a very serious problem. It certainly was in Tim's case. If hypoglycemia had been diagnosed and treated when he was a young child, many of his problems might have been eliminated. Instead, he spent his first sixteen years labeled with a behavior and psychiatric problem.

I counseled Tim on how to manage his diet so he would not have hypoglycemic episodes. I told him to stop eating all candy, cake, pies, and soft drinks. I told him to eat frequently and not to let himself get hungry. Although Tim understood and could recognize how hypoglycemia had affected his behavior and can now adapt his diet to prevent symptoms, he suffered so much emotional damage at the hands of modern medicine during his formative years that his complete recovery is in doubt. The medical system failed Tim for sixteen years. A simple change in the way he ate could have very dramatically changed his life for the better. Tim did not have ADHD; he had hypoglycemia.

Cody's story

As I was finishing this chapter, my pager went off. It was the mother of one of my patients, ten-year-old Cody. His mom sounded very upset. She and Cody had been in my office just yesterday. We had discussed how important it was for him to stay on his hypoglycemia diet. During testing in my office, Cody had reacted to many foods, showing marked changes in his personality. He also had a problem with low blood sugar if he did not eat often or ate sugar. When his mother called, she said that he had eaten two candy bars and ice cream at school and refused to eat anything else. He was completely out of control. He was going "ballistic," she said, and she feared that he might hurt himself or someone else. She was crying and didn't know what to do.

I explained that the most important thing at a time like this was to protect Cody from hurting himself or others. I told her that he might have to go to a hospital and that he may need to be medicated. Several different medications had been prescribed for Cody prior to his coming to my office. While taking them, his symptoms worsened. His mother did not want to use them. There is a time and a place for medications, I explained, and this might be one of those times. However, I told her that if she could get Cody to drink some Alka-Seltzer Gold, which can help neutralize food reactions, and to eat some protein, he might be all right. I told her to try and to call me right back. If the reaction Cody was having was from a food sensitivity, the Alka-Seltzer Gold (one tablet dissolved in water for age six to twelve, two tablets for age twelve and up) would probably help. If it were from hypoglycemia, the protein would help. Less than ten minutes passed before she called again. "He's fine," she said. "He drank the Alka-Seltzer Gold and ate a peanut butter sandwich. He's fine." (The peanut butter was free of sugar.) Hypoglycemia can be dramatic. Before Cody ate, the adrenaline was acting out, not Cody. We can blame the adrenaline for the behavior, but Cody must take the responsibility for eating the candy bars and ice cream. He can prevent these behavioral symptoms by eating the appropriate foods for his condition. Most of the children I see in my practice make responsible food choices once they see how certain foods affect them and know which foods to avoid.

CHAPTER 7

ALLERGIES AND SENSITIVITIES

Bart had been prescribed several different drugs for his behavior. None of them were effective. He was hospitalized for his behavior problems in a psychiatric institution twice by the age of five. When his insurance ran out, he was discharged. His symptoms continued.

Bart's parents brought him to see me, and I tested him for allergies and sensitivities. When I tested Bart for sensitivity to dairy products, his psychiatric symptoms exhibited themselves with a vengeance. Bart became aggressive, angry, and combative. He threatened to hit his mother and attempted to run out of the office. He kicked and tried to bite his mother when she stopped him. We had identified the irritant.

Allergies and sensitivities

Physicians know that it is very common for children labeled with ADHD to also have allergies. One pediatrician I know who considers himself to be an expert in the field of ADHD has been quoted frequently as saying that this association between ADHD symptoms and allergy is simply coincidence. How sad it is that

83

this physician's young patients will be labeled as ADHD and medicated because of their symptoms. This same physician is quick to acknowledge a set of symptoms for drug therapy yet ignores or discounts many of the same symptoms that could hold the key to, or solve, the whole problem. I believe we owe our patients more than a label and a drug.

To understand the allergy-testing procedure, one needs to understand the difference between an "allergy" and a "sensitivity." If you smell pepper and you sneeze, that's a sensitivity. If your body makes a particular antibody to pepper and you sneeze, then it is considered an allergy. Generally, allergists deal only with allergy problems where the body makes an antibody. Such problems are referred to as IgE allergy problems. Technically, IgE stands for "immunoglobulin E," which indicates the class to which the immunoglobulin belongs, and that it has different functions than the other immunoglobulins: G, M, A, and D.

Most allergists I have talked to tend to focus on the inhalants (pollens, dust, molds, dust-mites), which are the more common IgE allergies. Some of these allergists have told me that they believe that food allergies are not a very significant problem. They believe that a person must have an immediate reaction to the food in order to have a food allergy, in much the same way an IgE reaction usually occurs. A person with an IgE food allergy will have symptoms such as hives or throat constriction or skin rashes. They will recognize these symptoms as an immediate and direct reaction to a food just eaten.

One person I know who has an IgE allergy to peanuts finds that his throat will begin to close up if someone even opens a bag of peanuts in the same room. That kind of allergic reaction is a good example of an IgE allergic reaction. But for many of my patients, foods cause painful, difficult, and even serious symptoms that are not based in an IgE allergic reaction. A non-IgE food allergy affects them more subtly, and less immediately, than an IgE allergy would, but the effects are no less real or significant.

Researchers looking for IgE allergies to inhalants (e.g., trees, weeds, grasses, dust, molds) evaluated a group of infants who had a strong genetic predisposition to this type of allergy: both parents were highly allergic. When these infants were evaluated, they were found not to have the traditional IgE allergies to inhalants, but instead were found to have IgG (immunoglobulin G) antibody reaction to food. The researchers followed these children for several years and found that those who had specific IgG allergies to certain foods were much more likely to develop IgE allergies to certain inhalants later in life.[26] Perhaps if we address these IgG allergies earlier, we may not see our patients progress to IgE allergy problems. It appears that these IgE allergists may have been focusing on the wrong allergic reaction when they focus their treatment on IgE inhalant allergies instead of on IgG food allergies and/or sensitivities. There are many studies in the medical literature that show an association between foods eaten and behavior.[27–29]

As a medical student, I had the opportunity to spend several one-month rotations with various allergists. In one office in which the allergist restricted the practice to patients with IgE allergies, I saw the physician discount the symptoms of many people who suffered with classic allergic-type symptoms because they did not have the "IgE reaction." These patients are like the people who are sensitive to pepper. Although not IgE allergic, they do suffer from real symptoms as a result of something in their environment and they needed help.

If traditional allergists recognize only IgE allergies, I think that they should inform their patients of the limits that places on their diagnosis and care. As a student, I stood by silently and watched many people leave in frustration because, although they were truly suffering from a reaction to something in their environment, the patients were told that they did not have allergies and could not be helped.

Because of my experience and recognition that foods do in fact affect people, I focus a lot on food reactions in my practice. I don't care whether it's an allergy or a sensitivity, if the problem is interfering with the quality of a person's life, it deserves attention.

Symptoms of Allergies and Sensitivities

Vomiting/spitting up	Constipation/diarrhea
Colic	Hyperactive/overactive
Formula changes	Angry/hostile
Ear infections	Distractible
Dark circles under eyes	Fatigue
Congestion/runny nose	Learning problems
Coughing/wheezing	Had multiple antibiotics
Bed-wetting	Craves certain foods
Picky eater	Agitated/irritable after eating
Seasonal allergies	Seasonal behavioral changes
Hives/skin rashes/eczema	Stomachaches
Red earlobes/pink cheeks	Uncontrollable
Chronic infections	Sensitive
Headaches	

Determining if a person is sensitive or allergic to foods

There are several different approaches that can be taken to determine if someone is allergic or sensitive. I start with what is considered the "gold standard." This is the elimination-challenge diet.[30,31]

In this diet, you completely eliminate a food or combination of foods from five to seven days. Reading labels is extremely important for finding any ingredients that may contain any of the eliminated foods. After the elimination period, you reintroduce one food a day, on an empty stomach, and watch for signs and symptoms.

A second way to evaluate food allergies and sensitivities is to do a blood test called a RAST test. This test can determine through your blood if you have an IgE allergy to a food. This is definitely the safest route to go if you have any concerns that a life-threatening reaction could occur with an elimination-challenge diet. Remember, an IgE food reaction can cause hives or throat constriction, which can be life-threatening. You usually would already know if that were the case. If you have eaten a food at least twice and no serious consequences occurred, it is unlikely to occur in an elimination-challenge diet. However, if your child has a history of asthma, the asthma could worsen with the challenge. Always check with your doctor before trying any of these suggestions.

The third way to look for allergies and sensitivities is with skin testing. There are two different ways to do skin testing. One method is to test all the foods at one time by placing a drop of the allergen under the skin on the arm or the back. With this test, the doctor is looking for the reaction to the allergen on the skin. Will the skin turn red or grow a skin wheal (a red, irritated skin blister)?

The second skin test method tests one food at a time. This is done by placing one drop of a specific food allergen under the skin of the arm. By studying only one food at a time, the doctor and the patient can observe if a skin wheal grows and if any other types of reactions to the food occurs. Other common reactions often observed during testing when I test one food at a time in my office include changes in handwriting, heart rate, behavior, and breathing capacity. Many children with the symptoms of ADHD have a history of asthma, which can be incited during testing. Typical allergic symptoms like runny nose, watery eyes, and headaches can also occur. By testing one food at a time, you can learn very specifically which food causes which symptoms. If you place all of the allergens on the skin at one time and a reaction occurs other than a skin wheal, you would not know which allergen was the culprit. This is why I prefer this type of testing. If patients know what type of symptoms a food causes, they can decide whether to continue to eat the food, eliminate it from their diet, or be treated with allergy shots for the problem. The accompanying figure shows the effect apple has on this young man's handwriting. At the top right of the page is Mike's pretesting signature. What follows is Mike's handwriting samples as a result of being tested with different dilutions of the allergen, apple. As you can see, Mike lost control of his ability to write correctly. He began scribbling and writing backward. The final dose is the dose that brought Mike's handwriting back to normal. It was a weaker dose of the allergen apple. If Mike eats apple, it can affect his handwriting. If he takes an allergy injection of the dose of the apple allergen that cleared up his handwriting, he can eat apple without the negative effect.

The injections are given in the arm with a very small needle. Even children who are initially very scared of getting allergy tested find that the shots hurt very little. After receiving one or two injections, most children are very cooperative about getting the rest. I remember one little boy who refused to get out of his parents' car because he did not want to get a "shot." After experiencing the injections, he readily continued the testing.

The treatment of choice

I like to inform patients of their options and let them decide which choice works best for their life-style. Five years ago the pre-

NAME *Michael McCoy* DATE *11-8-94*

PULSE *18 Start*

20 *Pretesting*

MIKE

MiKe *MiKe*

SIGNATURE *MIKE*

PULSE *20* .05/1 003 *egg white*
7x7 mm

IM

SIGNATURE _____

PULSE *23* .05/2 003

SIGNATURE _____

PULSE *17* .05/1 003

MiKe

SIGNATURE _____

PULSE *20* 11 x 11 mm .05/1 024
wheal *apple*

MiK G

SIGNATURE _____

PULSE *23* 7x7 .05/2 024

MiKe

SIGNATURE _____

89

continued

Symptom Sheet

NAME *Michael McCory*   DATE 11-8-94

PULSE 19

9x9 .05/1   024

ODDMAMIKO SIGNATURE

PULSE 24

9x7 .05/2   024

MIKG   SIGNATURE

PULSE 25

.05/3   024

MIKe   SIGNATURE _____

PULSE _____

SIGNATURE _____

PULSE _____

SIGNATURE _____

PULSE _____

90

ferred treatment by parents was to eliminate the offending foods. Today, more people are choosing the antigen shots because they work more quickly and are more convenient than changing the diet.

Is it difficult to change a diet?

When patients ask me if it is difficult to change a diet, I say, "How bad is the problem?" If you have a child who is totally out of control from a food he or she is eating, it is much easier to change the diet (particularly when they are young) than it is to continue trying to cope with the problem. Doctors have told me that although they believe that a modified diet could be helpful, they do not recommend it because, in their estimation, to implement it could cause psychological damage to the child, and implementation is too difficult to accomplish.

But what about the psychological damage that can result from living with symptoms resulting from eating the foods to which they are sensitive? And consider the long-term psychological consequences of giving a child a psychiatric diagnosis and a potent mood-altering drug with many side effects. In Bart's case, was it less detrimental to place him in a psychiatric hospital for a behavior problem that was caused by something he was eating?

One pediatrician told me that he believes it is very unusual for children to react to foods, which is why he treats their symptoms with drugs like Ritalin instead of considering the option of dietary changes and discussing it with parents. In the next breath, he told me that he knows food reactions *do* happen because his own child reacts adversely to chocolate. Maybe it is not as rare as he thinks it is; he is just not looking.

An elimination diet for babies

A ten-month-old baby came to the office with a chronic skin rash that started when he was approximately three months old. Because the baby had been drinking a dairy-based formula and no other foods when the rash began, the dairy-based formula was highly suspect as the cause of the rash. Removing the formula and all other dairy from the diet temporarily would be one easy way to tell if the milk formula was the cause of the rash. For this age infant, the elimination of the food was the most preferred and cost-effective method of testing. In this case, the elimination of the dairy-based formula, and the substitution of a soy-based formula, eliminated the rash.

The elimination diet

There have been many excellent books written on how to implement the elimination-challenge and rotation diets. (See resources.) Basically here is what you do:

1. Eliminate all suspect foods completely from the child's diet. Suspect foods are those foods that a child eats every day and foods that the child loves and craves. These are the foods that the child would least like to give up. Your child is used to having this food and used to depending on it to modify the way he or she feels, much as many adults use coffee.

Dairy products and sweeteners are two of the most common foods I see that cause reactions. But any food at all can be the culprit. One child who "loves" salad actually became very hyperactive when he was tested on lettuce. This is very uncommon, however. Other foods that I often see reactions to are corn, wheat, yeast, orange, soy, peanut, beef, and chicken. You must read labels on foods carefully. When you begin to read labels, you will be amazed at how many foods contain hidden ingredients that you would not think would have any purpose in that particular food. When you read a food label you may not recognize that the dextrose in frozen potato products is actually a sweetener. Sweeteners and dairy products have many different names that may appear on a product label.

Sweeteners: sugar, honey, sucrose, glucose, maltose, fructose, dextrose, corn syrup, molasses (though Nutrasweet is not a true sweetener, I recommend avoidance of it as well).

Dairy: whey, caseinate, lactose, curd, cream, yogurt, cheese, cottage cheese, cream cheese, sour cream, butter, and some margarines

A food that is being eliminated must be eliminated completely. You cannot have "just a little bit." A little bit will ruin the accuracy of the test. Your child will have to take his lunch to school during this time and must understand that he is to eat no other food. I always tell the child that if some other food is eaten by accident, he must inform his parents. I tell the parents not to get angry—accidents happen. But the child needs to understand that if this occurs, the diet will have to start over at day one. This often motivates him to be very careful with the diet.

2. After eliminating the foods, you may see a worsening of behavior for two to three days. "Oh, great!" you say. But this is actually a good sign. This is the withdrawal stage. The food or foods may have given your child a lift; without it the craving is worsened. Her body wants the food, and she may become very irritable without it. It is very tempting to give the food to her to stop the irritable behavior, but don't. If she is older and chooses her own food at school and with friends, this is the time she may eat the food and not tell you.

The challenge

3. If your child successfully gets through this period, his or her behavior will improve by the fourth or fifth day. After two consecutive "good" days, you may start the challenge part of the diet. If good days do not occur, there are probably other foods that will need to be eliminated, or he has other sensitivities that will need to be evaluated, such as inhalant allergies (e.g., trees, weeds, molds, dust). You may have to find a physician who does provocation/neutralization allergy testing and treatment for more help.

To proceed with the challenge, select one offending food and feed it to your child on an empty stomach. Give only that one food. Watch for a reaction. The reaction can be physical (runny nose, wheezing, cough, stomach gas, stomach cramps, headache) or emotional (anger, anxiety, agitation, nervousness, hyperactivity). The reaction can occur immediately or it may take several hours. If a reaction occurs, do not give that food again. If the reaction is severe, you may give your child Alka-Seltzer Gold (Alka-Seltzer in the yellow box), one tablet for children under age twelve and two for twelve and older. Dissolve the tablet in a cup of water and let your child sip it. Alka-Seltzer Gold is the same as regular Alka-Seltzer but contains no aspirin. It will sometimes neutralize a food sensitivity reaction. If he does not react to the food, the food is considered to be safe, and he can continue to eat it. Your child may eat other foods that have not been removed from the diet during this time.

4. The next day, challenge another food in the same manner. If your child's reaction from the prior day has not subsided, wait another day until the reaction has subsided to challenge

the next food. Repeat each day until all foods have been challenged.

Rotation

5. When you have determined which foods must be avoided, you should start a rotation diet with all of the allowable foods. Foods take approximately four days to be completely digested. If you eat a food again while your body still has any part of that food in your system, you are more likely to develop a sensitivity to that food. For this reason no single food should be eaten more frequently than every fourth day. If you eat chicken on Monday, do not eat it again until Friday. You may eat foods from the same food family every other day. For example, wheat and corn are in the same food family. You may eat wheat on Monday, corn on Wednesday, and wheat again on Friday.

Monday:	Chicken	Wheat
Tuesday:		
Wednesday:		Corn
Thursday:		
Friday:	Chicken	Wheat
Saturday:		
Sunday:		Corn

A list of food and food families is found at the end of this chapter. The more diligent you are about eliminating the offending foods and rotating the rest, the better the results may be.

BART'S STORY: CONCLUSION

Removal of all dairy products from Bart's diet alleviated his psychiatric symptoms. Because all of his symptoms appeared to be related to his ingestion of dairy products, Bart could just stop eating dairy products. He did not have to take shots. However, if he had been sensitive to and reacted to many different foods, he would not have been able to easily eliminate all of the foods and probably would have taken shots so that he could continue to eat the foods. After Bart has kept all dairy from his diet for six months, he can try eating it again. If it still causes problems, he should then discontinue it for a year. If he has no problems when he adds dairy back into his diet, he should not eat dairy products more frequently than every four days. This will allow him to continue to eat dairy products without reacting. Bart did not have ADHD; he had a food sensitivity.

Behavior problems are often very obvious when they are a result of a food sensitivity and you do the elimination-challenge diet correctly. Attention problems alone are often more subtle and I believe often relate to learning differences.

Biological classification of foods and food families
(Food families are in bold)

Fungi: baker's yeast, brewer's yeast, mushroom
Grass: barley, corn, millet, oat, rice, rye, sugar, wheat, spelt, wild rice
Palm: coconut, date
Lily: asparagus, chives, garlic, leek, onion, shallot, aloe vera
Banana: banana, plantain, arrowroot
Walnut: walnut, pecan, butternut, hickory nut
Buckwheat
Pineapple

Goosefoot: beet, spinach, sugar beet, quinoa

Nutmeg: nutmeg, mace

Laurel: avocado, bay leaf, cinnamon

Mustard: broccoli, brussels sprouts, cabbage, cauliflower, collards, horseradish, kale, mustard greens, radish, turnip, watercress

Rose: apple, pear, almond, apricot, cherry, nectarine, peach, plum, blackberry, boysenberry, raspberry, strawberry

Legume: black beans, black-eyed peas, carob, fava beans, garbanzo beans, green beans, kidney beans, lentil, licorice, lima beans, navy beans, peas, peanut, soy

Citrus: grapefruit, lemon, lime, orange, tangerine

Cashew: cashew, mango, pistachio

Maple

Grape: cream of tartar, raisin, grape, wine, wine vinegar

Chocolate: cocoa, chocolate

Carrot: carrot, celery, cumin, dill, parsley

Heath: blueberry, cranberry

Mint: basil, marjoram, oregano, peppermint, rosemary, sage, thyme

Potato: eggplant, pepper, potato, tomato

Gourd: cucumber, melons, pumpkin, squashes

Composite: lettuce, safflower, sunflower seed, tarragon

Mollusk: clam, oyster, scallop, mussel

Crustacean: crab, crayfish, lobster, prawn, shrimp

Codfish: cod, haddock, pollack, whiting

Catfish

Dolphin: mahi-mahi

Mackerel: albacore, mackerel, tuna

Flounder: flounder, halibut, sole, turbot

Snapper

Salmon: salmon, trout species

Whitefish
Bass: white perch, yellow bass
Duck: duck, goose
Pheasant: chicken/eggs, pheasant, quail, cornish hen
Turkey
Swine: pork (bacon, ham, sausage)
Deer: deer, elk, moose
Beef: beef (gelatin, cow's milk products, cheese), veal, buffalo, goat, lamb

ened cereals are still the most popular breakfast item. Other favorites are pancakes or waffles covered with sweet syrup. Where are the nutrients in these foods? Lunch often goes uneaten. Sometimes a child will eat only dessert for lunch. Even if the child eats lunch, it may be processed-type foods or foods with little nutritional value. Most children I see do not eat vegetables or many fruits. As I said before, even if all the nutrients they need could still be obtained from a balanced diet, who in the world actually eats one?

In light of the many problems and concerns with the American diet, I believe that supplementing nutrients can help to make our children healthier, and as I've seen in my practice, the supplements make a major difference in how they feel and act. A list of nutrient suggestions follows.

If your child is unable to swallow pills, you can open capsules or crush a tablet, then place them in juice or in food like applesauce. If the nutrient is in an oil base, such as vitamin E or evening primrose oil, it can be rubbed on the skin. You are unlikely to find all of these nutrients and these dosages in one single capsule or tablet. However, the B vitamins might all be found in a B-complex form. I prefer that magnesium and calcium be given at different times of day, not together. Vitamin C and magnesium may cause loose bowels. If that should occur, decrease the dosage until the bowels are normal. Remember, just because a nutrient is good for you does not mean that more would be better. While most nutrients are water soluble and have no known toxicity or side-effects, some do have side-effects in large doses. Do not exceed recommended doses. Locate a physician in your area who knows about nutrition, and check with that physician before taking anything.

NUTRITIONAL SUGGESTIONS

(Always check with your physician before using)

Age	*0-2*	*2-6*	*6-12*	*12 and up*
B_1 (mg)	10	25	25	25
B_6 (mcg)	100	250	500	1,000
B_5 (mg)	5	10	25	50
Folate (mcg)	400	400	400	400
Calcium (mg)	200	500	500	500-1,000
Magnesium (mg)	100	150	200	100-400
Zinc (mg)	5	10	10	15
Beta carotene (IU)	5,000	10,000	25,000	25,000
Vitamin C (mg)	100	200	500	1,000
Vitamin E (IU)	10	50	100	200
Evening primrose oil (mg)	500	500	500	500
Flaxseed oil (tsp)	1	1	3	3

JIMMY'S STORY: CONCLUSION

Because of the history of drug and alcohol use by Jimmy's mother during her pregnancy, I had concerns that he might have nutritional deficiencies. I recommended that his guardians start Jimmy on the following nutrients (dosage and specific nutrients may vary from child to child):

Vitamin C 250 mg
Vitamin A 2,500 IU
Magnesium 250 mg
Evening primrose oil 500 mg
Vitamin E 200 IU

They returned a few weeks later to tell me what a dramatic difference the nutrients alone had made. His behavior was so much improved that they felt like he was a different child. Jimmy had become calm, disciplined, and lovable. Prior to the nutrient therapy, he would not hug his guardians or sit quietly in their laps. Now he would crawl into their laps and cuddle. Needless to say, they were very pleased with the results. And so was I. Jimmy didn't have ADHD; he had a nutritional deficiency.

Candida: a gut feeling that something is wrong

Candida albicans is a yeast that naturally grows in the intestinal tract. Though *Candida* usually should not be a problem, if the normal flora (good bacteria that help our foods break down properly) in the intestinal tract gets out of balance from the use of antibiotics or other medications or stresses, *Candida* has the opportunity to grow and get out of hand. The resulting imbalance can cause different symptoms in different people. Some of these symptoms can relate to behavior and the ability to learn.[35] So many children today have been prescribed multiple rounds of antibiotics for colds and ear infections. These antibiotics can throw off the natural balance in the intestinal tract. The antibiotics kill the good bacteria in the intestinal tract while killing the bad bacteria that is causing the illness. When my own children were young, their pediatrician routinely replaced, with a supplement, the good bacteria (*Lactobacillus acidophilus*) anytime he prescribed antibiotics. This practice appears to have been lost by most physicians today. An overgrowth of *Candida* can cause many health problems. In addition to the ones that traditional physicians see such as thrush and vaginal yeast infections, it can cause systemic problems throughout the body, which are often seen in immune compromised individuals.

Candida thrives and multiplies when we eat carbohydrates, especially the refined kind, like sugar. The child who has had antibiotic treatment and who eats the usual sugar-laden diet is the perfect host for an overgrowth of *Candida*. William Crook, MD, author of *The Yeast Connection*, reports that he has helped many children with their ADHD symptoms by treating the yeast in their digestive tract. I have found the same correlation in my practice as well. *Candida* is just one problem that can exist when the intestinal balance is altered. Other problems include bacteria overgrowth, parasites, malabsorption, and increased problems with food sensitivities. I have also found a correlation with the presence of parasites in the intestinal tracts of those children who have the most severe behavioral problems. Treating the yeast and/or the parasites can improve the ADHD symptoms.

Hyperthyroidism

A simple thyroid test will reveal if behavior and hyperactivity problems stem from a thyroid dysfunction. However, I have not seen this test routinely administered to children with these symptoms. I have not yet seen a child who had had his thyroid evaluated prior to his visit with me or prior to being placed on drugs for behavioral or hyperactivity problems. I routinely do this test though, and have had the test come back positive in a few individuals. A child who is hyperthyroid may have the same symptoms as a child who has been diagnosed with ADHD. In fact, I've seen Ritalin prescribed for several children who were actually hyperthyroid. While the number of thyroid disorders revealed is small, about six in a year, I still feel it is worth screening all children for this problem. If one child is spared an inappropriate drug and an inaccurate ADHD diagnosis when he or she actually had a thyroid problem, I feel it is worth the time and expense to do the study. Once the hyperthyroid diagnosis is made, I refer these children to an endocrinologist for treatment.

Feingold diet

The Feingold diet is another often overlooked remedy. Dr. Ben Feingold was a medical doctor who found that certain substances in foods, called salicylates, can affect behavior in some children. Salicylates are found in artificial colors and flavors, grapes, tomatoes, almonds, aspirin, and many other foods. He found that by removing all salicylate-containing foods from the child's diet, the behavior changed for the better. For the child who is salicylate sensitive, this diet can make a significant difference. Because Dr. Feingold's remedy to this problem was dietary instead of a drug, it did not fit the medical model and was not accepted in the medical community. However, many children with a sensitivity to salicylates are helped by the Feingold diet.[29,32] (See resources for more information.)

Vision therapy

For children who are tactile learners, vision therapy may be helpful. Vision therapy is a therapy usually performed by optometrists. There appear to be very few of them doing this type of therapy today. It was popular many years ago for the treatment of certain learning problems, particularly visual perception problems. It, too, did not fit the current medical model of using drugs to cover up symptoms, so it also was not accepted in the medical community. Vision therapy varies slightly from optometrist to optometrist, but it involves eye exercises to help with visual learning problems. It can be very effective. Children who are intelligent but do not like to read, who lose their place on the page, or reverse letters may benefit from vision therapy.

Auditory/listening therapy

For those with auditory learning problems, there are centers that deal with auditory learning programs. One I am familiar with is based on the theories of a man named Tomatos. Another is based on the theories of Berard. These centers understand the difference between hearing and listening. As I mentioned before, hearing is receiving sound, while listening is how the brain makes sense of what we hear. Listening must be learned. And just as we must learn to make sense of what we see (vision), we must also learn to make sense of what we hear (listening). Some children learn these skills automatically and others do not. (See Chapter 8 on learning differences.) Those who do not can be taught.

Most of these problems need a multidisciplinary approach. There is rarely one single treatment that will cure everyone of everything. I believe it is important to calm down the nervous system with diet, nutrients, and/or allergy and sensitivity treatment before beginning auditory or visual therapy. The therapies will be more effective and easier to accomplish if these other steps are achieved first.

Osteopathic manipulative therapy

Osteopathic manipulative therapy (OMT) is another effective treatment for some children with the symptoms of ADHD. The next chapter will explain OMT and the osteopathic profession.

CHAPTER 10

THE OSTEOPATHIC PHILOSOPHY

The Best-Kept Secret

My friend and mentor, Carlisle Holland, DO, used to say that osteopathic medicine is the best-kept secret in town, and if the public ever finds out about it, there won't be enough osteopaths to handle the demand. Leave it to a Harvard MD, Dr. Andrew Weil, to make osteopathy known to the world. In his book *Spontaneous Healing*, Dr. Weil spends an entire chapter on osteopathic medicine and specifically Dr. Robert Fulford, an osteopath who has retired from active practice but still teaches other physicians. I have been fortunate to have been trained by Dr. Fulford and know first-hand, in my practice, the advantages of his work.

Osteopathic physicians are real doctors, too

Osteopathic physicians are fully licensed physicians. They can write prescriptions, do surgery, and take any of the multitude of residencies in medicine, from neurosurgery to pediatrics. I used to be biased against osteopathic medicine. I thought DOs weren't "real" doctors. I thought they weren't as smart as "real" doctors or they would have gone to a "real" medical school (an MD school). But life has an interesting way of teaching us lessons. We may not always pay attention when we are being taught those lessons, but this one had my full attention. It was, of course, my daughter's illness that led me to osteopathic medicine. As I have said earlier in this book, I wouldn't have gone to an osteopath if my life depended upon it. But my daughter's life did, so I went. And what a surprise I got. The first osteopath I met was Dr. Gary Campbell. I was lucky, because Dr. Campbell represented all that was good about the osteopathic profession. And today it is very hard to find such a person.

The osteopathic advantage

When I found out about the osteopathic philosophy and the other differences between DOs and MDs, I realized I was wrong about my bias toward the osteopathic profession. The osteopathic medical school education is identical to the MD programs in all ways except two. To graduate from a DO school, you have to take more hours and actually learn more than MDs do. The osteopathic schools teach between one and two hundred additional hours about the musculoskeletal system. The MDs do not have this as a part of their education. The DO also studies the osteopathic philosophy.

With this extra time in learning about the musculoskeletal system and the osteopathic philosophy, the DO has the potential to see things differently than MDs do. First, they learn that there are other ways to help people besides drugs and surgery. Osteopaths learn to use their hands to heal with osteopathic manipulative therapy (OMT). There are many different manipulation techniques. Some may seem a little rough because they involve "popping" and "cracking" the bones and joints. Others are very gentle and involve the soft tissues such as the muscles and connective tissues. Sometimes manipulation is confused with chiropractic adjustments or massage. Though they are all similar, they are not the same. Osteopathic manipulation is a treatment using the physician's hands to help the body's nervous system, vascular system, and immune system work better.

Secondly, the osteopathic education focuses on the autonomic nervous system. This part of our nervous system is very important in understanding how our body works. The autonomic nervous system is that part of our nervous system that controls the functions of our body that we are not consciously aware of, including functions of our internal organs. It causes the eyes to dilate or constrict, our heart to beat faster and harder, the bronchioles in our lungs to dilate or constrict, our bladder to relax or contract, our skeletal muscles to have extra strength, and increases mental activity, just to name a few. The adrenaline I spoke about in the low blood sugar chapter is part of the autonomic nervous system. When adrenaline is released, it causes our eyes to dilate, our heart to beat faster and, if necessary, our muscles to have more strength.

There are many different ways to affect the autonomic nervous system. Eating sugar can be one way; becoming scared or fearful is another way. We can take drugs that will affect our autonomic nervous system, too. Just as there are many ways to release adrenaline and other autonomic nervous system chemicals, there are many ways to quiet them down. Taking drugs like Ritalin is one way; eating the right foods is another. Osteopathic manipulation is still another. I have had doctors tell me that they have positively affected 50 percent of the children they see with the ADHD diagnosis just by using OMT to affect the nervous system. When a doctor considers the autonomic nervous system in diagnosis and treatment, the patient is going to get a more holistic approach to the treatment. When you have a thorough understanding of the autonomic nervous system, it is easier to comprehend the different effects drugs have on the entire system, not just the part that is being treated with the drug. I feel these differences in our education give osteopaths the potential to be more open minded toward other medical models besides the drug model. This is why you often find osteopaths using a broader range of treatment modalities.

Not all DOs are osteopaths

Osteopathic medicine is actually a philosophy of medicine. It has been said that osteopathy is the only area of medicine that actually has a philosophy. This is what makes it so unique. But remember, not all DOs practice the osteopathic philosophy. Let me explain how I see the difference.

Everyone who graduates from an osteopathic medical school is a DO, a Doctor of Osteopathic Medicine. But just because they graduate from an osteopathic medical school doesn't mean they are osteopathic or practice the osteopathic philosophy. In fact some administrators in the osteopathic medical schools themselves do not practice the osteopathic philosophy and do not encourage the teaching of the philosophy. So I differentiate by saying that a person who graduates from an osteopathic medical school is a DO, whereas someone who practices the osteopathic philosophy is an osteopath. Most DOs are not distinguishable from MDs at all. So we have DOs (graduates of an osteopathic medical school) and osteopaths (practitioners of the osteopathic philosophy). Not all DOs are osteopaths and not all osteopaths are DOs. I have met many wonderful MDs who practice the osteopathic philosophy but have never seen the inside of an osteopathic medical school. The distinction between a DO and an osteopath is an important distinction when choosing a doctor. I have had patients who were pleased with my approach to medicine and believed, as I once did, that all osteopaths practiced the osteopathic philosophy. They told me that they wanted to switch all their medical care to DOs. I must warn you as I do them, not all DOs are osteopaths and not all DOs practice the osteopathic philosophy.

The osteopathic philosophy still works today

The osteopathic philosophy and profession was founded over 100 years ago by Dr. Andrew Taylor Still. Dr. Still, an MD, broke from the traditional medical model of the day and began a new model based on what he considered the best of all the medical practice options available. Andrew Taylor Still was a Kansas and Missouri doctor who became frustrated with the limitations of the medicine of his day. When he was unable to save the lives of his wife and several children, he began to look at medicine differently. He became interested in anatomy and how the nervous system worked. He wrote extensively about chemicals in the body that God had placed there. He said that "Man should study and use the drugs compounded in his own body."[18] His writings reflect that he had an understanding of how the body worked, about hormones and neurochemicals in the body. He wrote of these hormones and neurochemicals nearly one hundred years before modern medicine actually discovered them and named them. The Hippocratic medicine from which MDs take their Hippocratic Oath is actually a philosophy similar to the osteopathic philosophy. The health-oriented model of practicing medicine goes all the way back to Hippocrates. For a good historical review, the book *Third Line Medicine* is a good one to read.

There are many books written about the osteopathic profession for those of you who are interested in learning more. I am really proud to be an osteopath and practice the osteopathic philosophy. This philosophy is based on the concept that the body has an inherent ability to heal itself if given the proper tools to do so. In most osteopathic medical schools, the DOs who do osteopathic manipulation have been relegated the job of teaching the osteopathic philosophy. In many osteopathic medical schools, the osteopathic philosophy is not carried out or modeled anywhere else in the school with any consistency. These doctors who do osteopathic manipulation therapy (OMT) are actually specialists in osteopathic manipulation. Though they are usually the ones teaching the courses about the philosophy and are known for keeping the "osteopathic torch" alive, I don't think they are true osteopathic physicians, either. I would have to call them DOs, too. This is because they often limit their practices to OMT. The osteopathic philosophy, to me, is much, much more.

From my perspective, the only true osteopaths are those who incorporate the entire body and how it works into their practice. These individuals are often family practitioners who include OMT in their practice. They recognize the need for proper nutrition, exercise, and decrease in stress. They use drugs conservatively, and teach their patients how to stay healthy. It is hard to find these special physicians. Managed care makes them even harder to find.

OMT *saves lives*

Andrew Taylor Still was certainly a genius. There were many things that he understood and wrote about that medicine is just now recognizing. Osteopathic medicine and Dr. Still were ahead of their time. The public, then as now, was locked into a different medical model than Dr. Still was advocating. Dr. Still established his medicine in spite of the traditions of the day. Osteopathic medicine made a significant impact on public health in the first part of the twentieth century in this country. In 1918 and 1919, during the influenza epidemic, people were dying by the thousands. If the flu didn't kill them, pneumonia did. There were no antibiotics available to save these people. But those treated by osteopathic physicians with OMT did not die in the same high numbers as those treated by MDs.[47] OMT was an effective therapy for keeping people alive. People began flocking to Dr. Still and his disciples. Osteopaths became even more popular when that became known.

Antibiotics changed medicine

But soon antibiotics would be discovered. Everyone believed that antibiotics were the most important medical discovery ever. And they probably were. It was thought that antibiotics could cure anything and everything. The discovery of antibiotics ushered in a new era in medicine, the drug model, which still dominates today. People believed that with the use of antibiotics, they did not need the other medical modalities like OMT. Osteopathy lost its foothold in medicine. Osteopathy has celebrated its one hundredth birthday, and antibiotics and the drug model still reign supreme in the practice of medicine. But antibiotics are not the perfect answer we once thought they were. There are side-effects.

The antibiotic problem

With the abuse and overuse of antibiotics, we must develop stronger and stronger ones. With each stronger antibiotic comes a stronger, more resistant strain of bacteria that survives and causes us to need an even more powerful antibiotic. It has been said that soon we will not be able to produce an antibiotic strong enough to kill off the new strains of resistant bacteria.[34] We will then be back where we started, without effective antibiotic treatments. But we will still have OMT. OMT may save the day once again if that scenario actually occurs. And it probably will occur if doctors don't stop using antibiotics at inappropriate times. For example, 80 to 90 percent of all ear infections will heal entirely on their own, without the use of antibiotics.[37,38] There are studies that show that giving a child an antibiotic for an ear infection will actually cause the child to take longer to get over the infection and have more recurrences.[38] But this information doesn't stop pediatricians from prescribing antibiotics every time a child gets a red ear. Other studies show that the use of antibiotics for ear infections performed no better than actually doing nothing at all for the child's ear infection.[39]

OMT: *still good after all these years*

There are many studies in the osteopathic literature that indicate that OMT is beneficial for ear infections.[40–45] There is also medical literature that indicates that OMT is beneficial for the symptoms of ADHD.[46] As I explained earlier in this chapter, OMT affects the nervous system. Just as drugs like Ritalin affect the child's nervous system, OMT can do so as well.

It is difficult to acquire adequate funding to do the research with OMT. Remember, it is the drug companies who sponsor most of the medical research, and drug companies are not going to sponsor research that shows that OMT works better than drugs. So many people, including DOs, think of OMT as something that is used exclusively for back and neck pain. While it is very effective for those kinds of problems, it is also beneficial for so much more. Because of our knowledge of the autonomic nervous system and our ability to affect it through certain types of OMT, an osteopath can affect any or all parts of the body through OMT. In my office I teach parents how to do simple and gentle OMT treatments on their children to help relieve the fluid and pain that is associated with ear infections and other upper respiratory conditions. For parents who wish to learn these techniques, I have produced an easy to follow demonstration of these OMT treatments on video, which is available through my office. (See resources.)

OMT should be recognized as a major treatment modality in today's medical arena. It can be extremely valuable when used with other treatment modalities. Remember, the more tools we doctors have in our medical bag, the more people who can be helped. However, as long as doctors continue to be trained in the pill philosophy and drug model, osteopathic medicine will remain the best-kept secret in town.

EPILOGUE

I hope that the information in this book will be useful to you in your journey as you search for answers to help your children.

I see myself as an educator, sharing the information I find along the way. I share it with you in the hope that it will help to make your journey easier. No one should have to go to medical school to take care of his or her child.

RESOURCES

Programs from the Block Center

Learn-How-To-Learn with Buster B. Basset Hound™
> This comprehensive, at-home program is designed to enhance learning and attention skills in one fun, effective package.

See-Through Rainbow Book Marks: Feel-Good-About-Learning with Buster B. Basset Hound™
> This learning aid uses colors to help your child get in the mood to learn. The See-Through Rainbow Book Marks help your child read and retain the information through the use of colors to affect mood and calm the senses for enhanced learning ability.

Food-4-Kids: Learn-How-To-Eat with Buster B. Basset Hound
> This program assists meal planner and preparer to easily organize and implement the dietary plan. This program allows individual plans based on the child's food preferences.

Four-Day ADHD outpatient program at the Block Center
> For more information, call toll free: 1-888-Dr Block

Allergies and Sensitivities

Is This Your Child?
　　Doris Rapp, M.D.
Solving the Problem of Your Hard-To-Raise Child
　　William Crook, MD, and Laura Stevens
Hyper Kids
　　Lendon Smith, MD
Help for the Hyperactive Child
　　William Crook, MD
An Alternative Approach to Allergies
　　Theron Randolph, MD, and Ralph Moss, PhD

Nutrition

Super Immunity for Kids
　　Leo Galland, MD
Feed Your Kids Right
　　Lendon Smith, MD
Dr. Lendon Smith's Diet Plan for Teenagers
　　Lendon Smith, MD
Nutritional Influences on Illness
　　Melvyn Werbach, MD
Vitamin Bible for Your Kids
　　Earl Mindell

Candida-Yeast

The Yeast Connection
　　William Crook, MD

Osteopathy

Autobiography of A. T. Still
　　A. T. Still, DO

Philosophy of Osteopathy
    A. T. Still, DO
The Philosophy and Mechanical Principles of Osteopathy
    A. T. Still, DO
Frontier Doctor Medical Pioneer
    Charles Still, DO

Other Books

Third Line Medicine
    Melvyn Werbach, MD
Unlimited Power
    Tony Robbins

Feingold Association
P.O. Box 6550
Alexandria, VA 22306
(703) 768-FAUS

Sensory Integration International
1402 Cravens Avenue
Torrance, CA 90501-2701
(213) 533-8338

Lattitudes Newsletter
1120 Royal Palm Beach Blvd. #283
Royal Palm Beach, FL 33411

BIBLIOGRAPHY

1. *Diagnostic and Statistical Manual of Mental Disorders*, Fourth Edition, American Psychiatric Association, Washington, DC, American Psychiatric Association, 1994, pp. 83–85.
2. The adolescent outcome of hyperactive children diagnosed by research criteria I: An 8-year prospective follow-up study; Barkley, R. A., et al, *Journal of the American Academy of Child and Adolescent Psychiatry*, Vol. 29, No. 4, July 1990, pp. 546–556.
3. Stimulant medication used by primary care physicians in the treatment of attention deficit hyperactivity disorder; Wolraich, Mark, et al, *Pediatrics*, Vol. 86, No. 1, July 1990, pp. 95–101.
4. Is methylphenidate like cocaine? Volkow, Nora, et al, *Archives of General Psychiatry*, Vol. 52, June 1995, pp. 456–463.
5. Therapy for attention deficit hyperactivity disorder; Vinson, Daniel, *Archives of Family Medicine*, Vol. 3, May 1994, pp. 445–451.

BIBLIOGRAPHY

6. Treatment of attentional and hyperactivity problems in children with sympathomimetic drugs: A comprehensive review article, Jacobvitz, D., et al, *Journal of the American Academy of Child and Adolescent Psychiatry*, Vol. 29, No. 5, Sept. 1990.

7. Attention deficit disorder: A dubious diagnosis; The Merrow Report, Public Broadcasting, October 29, 1995.

8. Attention deficit hyperactivity disorder in adults; Bellak, Leopold, *Clinical Therapeutics*, Vol. 14, No. 2, 1992, pp. 138–147.

9. An open trial of guanfacine in the treatment of attention-deficit hyperactivity disorder; Hunt, Robert, et al, *Journal of the American Academy of Child and Adolescent Psychiatry*, Vol. 34, No. 1, 1995, pp. 50–54.

10. Using psychostimulants to treat behavioral disorders of children and adolescents; Dulcan, Mina, *Journal of Child and Adolescent Psychopharmacology*, Vol. 1, No. 1, 1990, pp. 7–19.

11. *20/20* Show, ABC Television, October 27, 1995.

12. Ritalin Brochure, Ciba-Geigy, 1995.

13. *An Alternative Approach to Allergies*, Randolph, Theron, M.D. and Moss, Ralph, Ph.D., Harper and Row Publishers, Inc., New York, 1989, pp. 83–84.

14. Cognitive side-effects of antiepileptic drugs; Meador, Kimford, *Canadian Journal of Neurological Sciences*, 21(30):s12, 1994, Aug.

15. *Physicians' Desk Reference*; Arky, Ronald, M.D., Medical Consultant, Medical Economics, Montvale, New Jersey, 1996, pp. 412–413, 674–675, 848–849, 856–857, 919–923, 1526–1527, 2474–2476.

16. Enhanced adrenomedullary response and increased susceptibility to neuroglycopenia mechanisms underlying adverse affects of sugar ingestion in healthy children; Jones, Tim, et

al, *Journal of Pediatrics*, Vol. 126, No. 2, Feb 1995, pp. 171–177.

17. *Healthy School Handbook*; Miller, National Education Association, Washington, DC, 1994, pp. 121–134.

18. *The Autobiography of A. T. Still*, Still, A. T., A. T. Still, D.O., Kirksville, Missouri, 1908.

19. Sugar intolerance: Is there evidence for its effects on behavior on children; Wolraich, Mark, *Annals of Allergy*, Vol. 61, Dec 1988, pp. 58–61.

20. Reactive hypoglycemia; Hofeldt, Fred, *Endocrinology and Metabolism Clinics of North America*, Vol. 18, No. 1, March 1989, pp. 185–201.

21. Hypoglycemia in infants and children; Haymond, Morey, *Endocrinology and Metabolism Clinics of North America*, Vol. 18, No. 1, March 1989, pp. 211–253.

22. The contribution of the autonomic nervous system to changes of glucagon and insulin secretion during hypoglycemic stress; Havel, Peter and Taborsky, Gerald, *Endocrine Reviews*, Vol. 10, No. 1, 1989, pp. 332–350.

23. Sugar "allergy" and children's behavior; Mahan, Kathleen and Chase, Mabel, *Annals of Allergy*, Vol. 61, Dec 1988, pp. 453–458.

24. Histamine: An early messenger in inflammatory and immune reactions; Falus, András and Merétey, Katherine, *Immunology Today*, Vol. 13, No. 5, 1992, pp. 154–156.

25. Neuropeptides, mast cells and allergy: Novel mechanisms and therapeutic possibilities; Goetzl, E. J., et al, *Clinical and Experimental Allergy*, Vol. 20, Suppl. 4, 1990, pp. 3–7.

26. Relationships between IgG1 and IgG4 antibodies to foods and the development IgE antibodies to inhalant allergens. II. Increased levels of IgG antibodies to foods in children who

subsequently develop IgE antibodies to inhalant allergies; Calkhoven, P. G., et al, *Clinical and Experimental Allergy*, Vol. 21, 1991, pp. 99–107.

27. Controlled trial of hyposensitization in children with food-induced hyperkinetic syndrome; Egger, J., et al, *Lancet*, Vol. 339, May 1992, pp. 1150–1153.

28. Dietary replacement in preschool-aged hyperactive boys; Kaplan, Bonnie, et al, *Pediatrics*, Vol. 83, No. 1, Jan 1989, pp. 7–17.

29. Foods and additives are common causes of the attention deficit hyperactive disorder in children; Boris, M. and Mandel, F., *Annals of Allergy*, Vol. 72, No. 5, May 1994, pp. 462–468.

30. Double-blind placebo-controlled food challenge (DBPCFC) as an office procedure: A manual; Bock, S., et al, *Journal of Allergy and Clinical Immunology*, Dec 1988, pp. 986–997.

31. Sixteen years of double-blind, placebo-controlled food challenge (DBPCFC); *Pediatric Notes*, Gellis, Sydney, M.D., Editor, Vol. 14, No. 44, Nov 1990, p. 176.

32. Synthetic food coloring and behavior: A dose response effect in a double-blind, placebo-controlled, repeated measures study; *Journal of Pediatrics*, Rowe, Katherine and Rowe, Kenneth, Vol. 125, No. 5, Nov 1994, pp. 691–698.

33. Attention deficit hyperactivity disorder and thyroid function; Weiss, Roy, *Journal of Pediatrics*, Vol. 123, Oct 1993, pp. 539–545.

34. Germ warfare; Sprovieri, John, *The DO*, Vol. 37, No. 3, March, 1996, pp. 40–48.

35. *Solving the Puzzle of Your Hard-To-Raise Child*, Crook, William and Stevens, Laura, Professional Books, Random House, New York, 1987, pp. 129–132.

36. New mechanisms of bacterial resistance to antimicrobial agents; Jacoby, George and Archer, Gordon, *New England Journal of Medicine*, Vol. 324, No. 9, Feb 28, 1991, pp. 601-612

37. Pediatric approach to the diagnosis and management of otitis media; Kempthorne, Jill and Giebink, G., *Otolaryngologic Clinics of North America*, Vol. 24, No. 4, Aug 1991, pp. 905–929.

38. Abuse and timing of use of antibiotics in acute otitis media; Diamant, M. and Diamant, B., *Archives of Otolaryngology*, Vol. 100, Sept 1974, pp. 226–232.

39. Choosing the right therapy for acute otitis media; English, G., *The Journal of Respiratory Diseases*, July 1985, pp. 93–100.

40. Manipulative therapy of upper respiratory infections in children; Purse, F., *Journal of the American Osteopathic Association*, Vol. 65, May 1966, pp. 964–972.

41. Infections of the ear, nose and throat; Blood, Harold, *Osteopathic Annals*, Vol. 6, No. 11, Nov 1978, pp. 14–18.

42. An integrated osteopathic treatment approach in acute otitis media; Pintal, W. and Keutz, M., *Journal of the American Osteopathic Association*, Vol. 89, No. 9, Sept 1989, pp. 1139–1141.

43. Osteopathic manipulation in eye, ear, nose and throat disease; Ruddy, T. J., *American Academy of Osteopathy Yearbook*, 1962, pp. 133–140.

44. Osteopathic manipulative therapy as a primary factor in the management of upper, middle and para respiratory infections; Schmidt, Ida, *Journal of the American Osteopathic Association*, Vol. 81, No. 6, Feb 1982, pp. 382–388.

45. Management of ENT problems; Woods, Donald, *Osteopathic Annals*, Vol. 8, No. 5, May 1980, pp. 31–41.

46. Effect of osteopathic medical management on neurological development in children; Frymann, V., et al, *Journal of the*

American Osteopathic Association, Vol. 92, No. 6, June 1992, pp. 729–744.

47. Death statistics reveal comparative values of osteopath and drug treatments; *Osteopathic Physician*, Vol. 34, Dec 1918, pp. 1–2.

INDEX